"Shine the flashlight right here on the chain," he instructed.

Lifting a shaky arm, she did as she was asked, illuminating the rusty rings of iron.

Bob examined them, drawing closer to the German shepherd. Although the puppy had lost its courage and scampered away beneath the larger dog, the German shepherd stood there patiently, its shoulder still bleeding as Bob tried to free him.

"The bastard didn't even put a collar on him," Bob commented, lifting his head to look at Rose. "He just wrapped the chain around the base of the dog's neck, put a lock at the end of it and left the animal here to die."

Rose swallowed hard.

"For all we know, that puppy over there saved this shepherd by bringing him food. It would certainly explain how he survived this long."

"God, Bob. Can we free him?"

"I'm going to try." He began cutting one of the links farthest from the shepherd.

Rose couldn't help staring at the large dog as the sound of screeching metal resounded around them. Large brown eyes met hers in the darkness and held her gaze. That gaze was so powerful and so full of life, Rose almost burst into tears. Who could do such a thing? Who could take a life, be it in the form of an animal or human, and treat it with such cruelty?

CANINE CAPER

Real-life Tales of a Female Pet Vigilante

ROSE BLOCK
AND
DELILAH AHRENDT

BERKLEY BOOKS, NEW YORK

CANINE CAPER

A Berkley Book / published by arrangement with
New Horizon Press

PRINTING HISTORY
New Horizon hardcover edition published in 2001
Berkley edition / November 2002

Copyright © 2001 by Rose Block and Delilah Ahrendt
Book design by Julie Rogers
Cover design by The Great American Art Company
Cover photograph by Photodisc

Visit our website at
www.penguinputnam.com

ISBN: 0-425-18710-1

BERKLEY®
Berkley Books are published by The Berkley Publishing Group,
a division of Penguin Putnam Inc.,
375 Hudson Street, New York, New York 10014.
BERKLEY and the "B" design
are trademarks belonging to Penguin Putnam Inc.

PRINTED IN THE UNITED STATES OF AMERICA

10 9 8 7 6 5 4 3 2 1

❖❖ Contents

Authors' Note   vii

Acknowledgments   ix

Prologue   1

1. Somebody, Help!   4
2. Abandoned   12
3. The Dog Rescuers   18
4. Emergency Measures   23
5. Chance for Survival   31
6. A Form of Lunacy   38
7. Nightmares   45
8. The Smell of Death   54
9. Looking for Shelter   60
10. A Small Deposit   66
11. Eerie Silence   77
12. Sleepless Nights, Tortured Days   90
13. Strange Homecoming   102

14. Dump Dog Month   112

15. Hearts, Flowers and a Black Dog   117

16. Lost Valentine   132

17. Just Another Dog   138

18. Doggy Pickup   145

19. A Hurt Dog, a Future Pet   155

20. Billy/Butch   170

21. Through Wind, Rain and Snow   178

22. Humane Aid and Small Miracles   191

23. Deadly Dogfight   201

24. Murder and Animal Control   212

25. "Shoot on Sight"   219

26. Cruelty Strikes Home   227

27. An Animal Lover   235

    Epilogue   241
    Afterword   246

❖ ❖ Authors' Note

This book is based on the real experiences of Rose Block and those of her family. The personalities, events, actions and conversations portrayed within the story have been largely taken from her memory and personal papers.

Some of the dialogue represented in this book was reconstructed from her memory and/or the memories of the participants. A few of the scenes depicted have been reconfigured and enhanced for clarity and dramatic impact drawing on sometimes differing memories and versions of papers and interviews.

In order to protect privacy and because of possible legal ramifications, Rose does not use her married surname or actual locale. Also, some other characters have been given fictitious names, addresses and descriptions and identifying details have been altered. With one exception, Royce, who is a composite, all of the people in the book are actual.

Acknowledgments

I'd like to dedicate this book to a special dog named Homer. Even though he is now in a loving home, he finds it difficult to trust anyone. He would rather run out into oncoming traffic than into a group of people. Each and every day you remind me, Homer, why I set out to write this book. I would like to thank my husband, Marc, who brought this incredible story to my attention, and supported me through all the unexpected obstacles that came my way. I want to thank my father, Richard, who taught me to love reading, which, in turn, taught me to love writing. And last but not least, I want to thank Melissa, Terri and Leah, my one and only critique group, for your unwavering support not only through this project, but throughout all my projects.

—DELILAH AHRENDT

I'd like to dedicate this book to all the neglected, abused and/or starved dogs who are still lingering on their chains, unable to free themselves from their "owners." These dogs are probably the very reason the term "underdog" came about.

—ROSE BLOCK

❧❧ Prologue

One cloudy December morning, and already thirty minutes late to work, Rose Block saw him, a tiny black, dusty twig of an animal wandering alone, sniffing the road, searching. She was sure the puppy was looking for food. His caved sides told of hunger.

Slowing her car, she stared at the emaciated animal, wondering how much longer he had until he starved to death.

It was then Rose knew she had to help the poor creature. Who else would?

And so it began. Almost without thinking, she pulled over her car and jumped out, leaving the engine running. Late or not, she couldn't just drive by.

"Here puppy," she called out, stepping toward the curb.

He scampered away.

"Damn." She quickly went back to the car and yanked the keys from the ignition. If she was going to go after the pup, she couldn't leave her car running. She couldn't leave her purse, either. Not in this neighborhood. She grabbed her purse along with the wrapped sandwich she had brought with her for lunch. Perhaps she could entice him.

Burned out, graffiti-stained buildings and gutted cars surrounded her. The only reason she drove through the southeast section of Dalton City that morning was because it was the quickest way of getting to work. She knew it could be dangerous for a woman to be out alone on these deserted streets, but she had to get that dog.

Rose wasn't prepared for a chase, especially a chase that led her down back streets and then an alley, but somehow she followed, keys and sandwich in hand, her purse slung around her neck. She kept stumbling on her high heels, trying to keep up while throwing bits of the sandwich in front of her trying to get the pup's attention, before finally seeing the dog hurry around the side of a sooty clapboard house and into the backyard. There, something else was waiting for her. Something more sizeable than a puppy. She froze.

A huge German shepherd stared at Rose with anxious eyes. Although the grossly starved dog appeared frightened and confused by her presence, she saw it could do nothing to harm her. The poor creature could neither move forward nor back, so tightly was the animal chained to a rusted and severely dented oil drum that was twice its size.

And that shoulder! Rose swallowed the acid taste of vomit that threatened her clenched throat. The dog's shoulder was nearly twice its normal size, misshapen and looked like it had been stabbed. The wound oozed thick blood and large amounts of cream-colored pus mixed with the fur. On the flat yellow grass beneath the German shepherd were pools of crusty blood.

The dog stared at Rose as if it had never seen a human face before. Licking its chops caused a string of saliva to hang down the side of its mouth. Distrust filled its brown, humanlike eyes, its large head still half-cocked, its left ear brushing up against the rusted oil drum.

Rose stepped closer, the fear she felt diminishing with each passing moment. What owner would allow his or her dog to get to such a pitiful and neglected state? Although the shepherd was quite large, it was so thin she could see every rib pushing against its side each time the dog breathed.

At the base of the animal's neck, where the chain was wrapped, there was little fur left and patches of red raw skin shone from beneath the rusted links. The dog was leaning into the dented oil drum to which it was attached. The animal had no other means of resting.

Rose gazed at the dog's infected shoulder. She wondered if it had received the wound fighting with other dogs, but the more she looked at it the more she realized it was too deep and too clean-cut. No animal she knew of could create a slice like that. It looked like it was done with an ax.

She paused, horrified by the thoughts that were going through her head. Only humans knew how to use axes. A sick bastard of a human, she thought as a wave of nausea roiled her stomach once again.

Suddenly, a small black head peered out from the other side of the oil drum. The puppy! The same puppy she had chased into the yard, hoping to rescue. There was something about the small, black face that was faintly familiar. Instantly, she remembered Valentine, the tiny cat she had befriended long ago. Only now, she realized, the shepherd was the one that needed rescuing.

The young dog ducked from sight, only to reappear on the other side of the drum. He looked at Rose with large frightened eyes and then slid between the shepherd's hind legs, crawling into the pool of dried blood.

The shepherd shook its head, then went back to staring at Rose. It snarled protectively and Rose felt she knew why. The shepherd was trying to take care of the puppy. She must be the puppy's mother!

Rose drew back, trying to decide what to do. She had to help them, but how?

❧ ❧ Chapter 1

Somebody, Help!

Rose frantically looked around. Silent brick buildings loomed above her. Nine A.M. in southeast Dalton City, Michigan, yet one might have thought it was the middle of the night. There was no one around. The backyard she stood in was as neglected and pathetic as the dogs before her.

High, frost-killed grass brushed up against her nylon-covered legs and broken beer bottles lay strewn everywhere, along with dozens of wrappers from burger places. Cigarette butts lay in neat little piles here and there, as if someone occasionally visited just to deposit their ashtray.

And the house behind her? All the windows on the dilapidated yellow house were broken, pane after pane, with only a few bearing jagged edges of glass that hung like torn curtains. And on almost every windowsill stood an empty beer bottle or two—replacing the idea of flowerpots altogether.

The yellow clapboard sides were spray-painted with various symbols, unreadable words and profanity. On the roof, some shingles were torn up and tossed on the ground, while other sections hung from the lopsided gutter. A ripped up mattress dangled from one of the second story windows, threatening to fall out at any moment.

What was more horrifying to Rose than the defiled house was knowing that the shepherd behind her had been imprisoned here to starve and slowly bleed to death.

Dressed in black heels and a business suit, Rose felt very out of place.

The dog that had dramatically altered her plans for the day was barking wildly, showing crude yellow teeth and black gums as she tried to pull away from the drum. Although the tone of the bark hadn't changed, it wasn't as frightening as at first. It was clear now that the dog was simply communicating with her. The German shepherd was barking as if to say, *Get lost or get me some help, lady!*

"Okay, okay," she murmured reassuringly, pulling her cell phone from her purse. "I'm going to try to get you the help you need. And you definitely need help."

What was she going to do? She had to think. Think! Ah, yes! The Humane Society should be able to help!

She got the number from Information and dialed it with a quivering fingertip. She waited as it rang and rang and rang.

"Shouldn't someone be answering this?" she impatiently cried, shifting the phone to her other ear.

"The Humane Society. How can I help you?" a female voice finally said.

"I need you to send someone down here right away. Or, better yet, send an ambulance. An ambulance would be much better."

"What is this concerning, Miss?" the woman nonchalantly asked.

"A—a dog. There's a dog that really needs help. She's chained to an oil drum, and she's cut to the bone, which I think is broken, and she's bleeding and—"

"Is the dog dead, Miss?"

Rose frowned. Why would she be calling if the dog was dead? "No, of course not."

"I'm sorry, but we currently don't have a pick-up service."

"What do you mean?" Rose exclaimed, sputtering into the receiver. "I need someone to come out and help me help this dog. I don't even know how long it's been out here or if—"

"I understand how you feel, but—"

"No, you *don't* understand how I feel!" Rose blustered. "You're not out here with a dog that's bleeding to death. I need help and I need it *now*!"

"I'm sorry. We don't take calls like this anymore, Miss."

"Well, what kind of calls do you take? This is an emergency! If I wanted information, I would have called an operator for the telephone company. I need you to send someone over right away!"

"I'm sorry. We can't help you," the woman said in a dry monotone. "Call Anti-Cruelty. They take care of that sort of stuff."

"But can't you—"

"Call Anti-Cruelty, Miss."

Rose ground her teeth. "Even if I wanted to, I don't have their number."

"It's 555-2000," the woman quickly offered. "They'll help you."

Rose wished at that very moment she could have reached through the phone and slugged her for not being more helpful. Then again, Anti-Cruelty sounded like an organization that would be more well-suited to handle this type of situation. She dialed the number and waited impatiently as it rang and rang.

"Anti-Cruelty. This is Dare," a female voice finally acknowledged.

"Dare!" Rose exclaimed, her nervousness showing. "I don't know what you're capable of doing for me, but please tell me you can help!"

There was silence for a moment. "Okay...what can I help you with?"

"I'm in southeast Dalton City on Chester Street between Bell and Kenneth Streets. I found a dog, or rather, two dogs that need help. The one I'm really worried about is the mother. Some sicko must have put an ax or something to the dog's shoulder. Anyway, it's bleeding, it's infected and the dog looks like it hasn't been fed in—"

"I understand," the woman calmly interrupted. "So where did you find the dog?"

Rose looked toward the animal who was still staring at her with distrust. "I found her attached to an oil drum. I'm pretty sure it's a she. There's a puppy clinging to her side."

"Did you say the dog was attached to an oil drum?"

"Yes. She's chained to an oil drum."

"I see. And where is she chained?"

Rose was now growing impatient. With each moment, the dog had less of a chance of surviving. "I already told you! I'm on Chester Street between Bell and Kenneth in southeast Dalton City!"

"I understand," the woman reassured her. "But is the dog on someone's property?"

"I suppose it's someone's property, but clearly the dog's been abandoned."

"I'm sorry, but we can't help you."

Rose almost let out a piercing scream. "What do you mean you can't help me? I was just transferred over to you! You—you have to help me! This dog is going to die if you don't!"

"If you're on someone's property, we can't get involved," the woman explained. "That's the law."

Rose snapped her body toward the house behind her and once more took in the broken windows and the torn-up roof. Dozens of dried eggshells and their contents clung to one wall, decorating the abandoned masterpiece perfectly.

"The only things that could possibly be living in the house I'm looking at are rats," Rose retorted. "And correct me if I'm wrong, but rats don't own homes. I assure you nothing human is on the property. Now, *please* say you'll help me!"

"I'm sorry, Ma'am. If the dog was on the street or somewhere in a park or any other place of public domain, we could step in right away. But when a dog is chained and in someone's backyard, it means that the dog belongs to someone and we just aren't allowed to get involved in that sort of stuff."

Rose felt the heat in her cheeks rising. "But I can't get the dog out without help. There's no way I can manage to free her from the oil drum she's chained to."

"I'm sorry we can't help you, but—"

"Oh God, no. Please. Please don't do this," Rose pleaded, not knowing how else to convince the woman. She had to make her understand. "I need help. And I can't leave this dog. I—I just can't leave. It would be worse than what was already done to her."

"I understand and it sounds like you're very concerned. However, all I can do for you is give you the number of a nearby animal shelter. You'll have to call them."

Rose felt like crying. "Please, couldn't you make an exception this once? The dog is in terrible shape."

"I see all kinds of animals coming in through our doors. Believe me, I understand. But we can't help you with this one. Call five-five-five, six-one-eight-nine."

"Five-five-five, six-one-eight-nine," Rose agitatedly repeated.

"That's right. They'll help you. I promise."

Hoping this would be the answer to her plight, Rose quickly thanked her and hung up. She had no choice but to make the call. She only hoped this would be her last. She repeated the number out loud so she wouldn't forget it and punched it into her phone just as fast.

While the phone rang in her ear, the dog's bark changed to a howl, now exhibiting great pain. Rose winced and tried not to cry. She wished with all her heart that she could take the animal's pain, if but for a moment, to make her feel at peace.

"Animal Life. This is Frank."

"Frank, hi," Rose said praying she would get a better reaction from the man. "I've got some real trouble here. I'm hoping you can help me."

"Sure. What's the problem?"

She took a shaky breath. "I found a dog and it needs

medical attention right away. Someone cut its shoulder badly and—"

"I'm sorry, but I can tell you right now that we wouldn't be able to help you," the man said, making Rose's heart drop in misery. "We aren't currently staffed to take care of such extreme cases."

"'You aren't currently staffed,'" Rose repeated as if she didn't understand what the words meant. Why wasn't anyone able to help her? Surely there had to be someone. She was taking time off from work to help this dog and people who were supposedly PAID to help animals weren't doing what they were supposed to!

"Please, Frank," she pleaded. "You have to help me. No one else will. Do you understand? I've already talked to two other organizations and they keep pushing me off on someone else. You have to help this dog. Do you understand? You have to!"

"I can't help you," the man insisted. "We're a proactive organization that fights for better treatment of animals. You'll have to try an agency that specializes in these situations."

"These situations," she murmured to herself as Frank hung up. But who? No one wanted to help. She would have to call her husband, Bob, even though he had never been an animal lover, never even wanted pets. But would he come? They hadn't been getting along as well as they once had. There were no fights, only a growing silence between them. Nevertheless, she would have to call him.

God, what if he left the house to go somewhere? What if she couldn't get him? Or worse, what if he refused to come? No. She couldn't think that way. She had to reach him. He had to come.

"Yeah?" he answered, his voice muffled as though he was eating something.

"Bob?" Rose let herself grow hopeful, clutching the phone closer to her ear and mouth as if that were going to make him feel compassion for the dog.

"I need your help badly." Her words rushed together. "I

was on my way to work when a puppy ran into the road and led me to this huge German shepherd, who is chained to an oil drum and bleeding."

Rose heard a shuffle, as if Bob was changing the way he was holding the phone. "Aren't you supposed to be at work?"

"Forget work. I've been trying to get the authorities to help me, but no one wants to get involved. The German shepherd is in really bad shape. I mean really bad shape," she emphasized. "Its shoulder looks broken and, worst of all, it's chained so tightly it can't lay down without choking itself. It's horrible. Absolutely horrible."

She paused for breath.

"That doesn't sound good. How long do you think it's been out there like that?" Bob asked.

Rose hesitated. She couldn't possibly fathom the answer to that. The dog was still alive. If it had been here for more than a week, it would be a miracle if it had survived. "I'd say about a week."

"Can you see the bones on its sides?"

She nodded, then realized he couldn't see her. "Yes."

"Badly?"

"Badly."

"It's probably been there a month. Maybe even longer."

Rose took in a sharp breath and jerked toward the dog which was growing more restless. If it had been chained to the oil drum for more than a month, that would explain why it was so nervous around her. Then again, someone also tried to stab it and had surely broken the poor thing's shoulder. Perhaps the dog was thinking she was here to finish the job. "Please. I know you don't like animals the way I do, but will you come?"

Silence filled the air. Finally, he said, "Alright, Rose. I don't like this, but I'll be there as soon as I throw on some clothes. Where are you anyway?"

"I'm in southeast Dalton City, on Chester Street between Kenneth and Bell. I'm in the backyard of a yellow house. I'd give you the address, but I didn't see one coming in. It's the only yellow house on the block. The rest are brick buildings."

"That neighborhood? I don't believe this. Listen, I want you to stand out in front of the house where I can see you."

"Right."

"I'll be there in twenty minutes. You be out front."

"Right." She forgot to thank Bob as she hung up. She was in a state of awe and shock that her husband was coming to help her. They had been living separate lives lately, what with him on the road all the time. "Maybe things aren't that bad between us," she murmured, wiping away a tear.

Her heart filled with hope as she stepped a foot closer to the suffering mother and her pup. "We're going to help you. I promise." She headed toward the front of the house. "I won't be long," she said softly, wishing the dog understood. "We'll set you free. I promise."

She walked back down the alley and stood near the curb. As she waited for Bob, her mind spun backwards.

❖❖ Chapter 2

Abandoned

A small girl silently sat on the cold basement floor of an orphanage, chewing on her fingernails. She always bit her nails when she was sent to the basement, which lately was more often than not. It wasn't her fault. She wanted to be outside, playing in the snow, not cleaning toilets.

When she had no more nails left to chew, she wrapped her arms around herself and rocked back and forth. She hated the basement. It was cold, dark and desolate. But the loneliness was the worst part of it.

She closed her eyes and tried to sing her loneliness away. "Raindrops on roses and whiskers on kittens, bright copper kettles and warm woolen mittens. Brown paper packages tied up with string, these are a few of my favorite things..."

Squeak. Squeak.

She opened her eyes and looked around. What was that? A rat? She shivered.

Squeak. Squeak. There it was again! The sound became louder. It almost sounded as if it was coming from outside.

Her eyes traveled to a small window covered with frost

that glittered in the morning light. A black cat with huge green eyes was scratching at the window as if it wanted to come in.

She looked back at the locked door of the basement. They had strict rules about animals in the orphanage. She would get an even worse punishment if she were caught with one. The cat continued to paw at the window.

She slowly rose from the position to which she had been sentenced for the next five hours and quietly stepped toward the window.

Standing on tiptoes, she stared with wonder at the cat on the other side. The girl loved animals, especially dogs and cats, and this one was without a doubt the most beautiful creature she had seen in all seven years of her life. But it looked cold and miserable.

"Just like me," she murmured.

Seeing the latch on the narrow rectangular window, she touched a shaky hand to it. It was like touching ice.

She looked back at the locked door one last time, then gripped the latch and yanked it. The window squeaked open and the tiny cat inched closer.

"Here, little cat," she whispered, offering her hand. "Come here. Come on."

"Meow."

Without hesitation, the cat squeezed through the small opening of the window and the girl was able to gather up the frozen ball of fur. Quickly, she closed the window.

Pressing the creature to her chest to keep it warm, she hurried back to the spot where she was supposed to be sitting.

The cat purred in her arms as she rubbed his head and she smiled. If only she could keep him.

Perhaps she could hide him here in the basement. She came down often enough and would be able to feed him and play with him.

She kissed his small head, her lips absorbing some of the melting snow on its coat. "I'll call you Valentine, seeing as it's tomorrow," she whispered into his ear. "I love Valentine's Day and you're the best valentine I could get."

Suddenly, the door behind her opened. Rose froze in terror.

"What do you have there, Rose?" the woman called out, her steps echoing as she strode toward the girl.

The girl scrambled to hide the cat behind a box but failed to move fast enough.

She cried out as the woman snatched the cat away. "Please, Miss Roberts," she pleaded. "It's awfully cold outside."

The stocky woman dangled the small cat from her fingers as if it were a rat and walked over to the window. "You know the rules about animals. We have enough problems without them. You being one of them."

With that, Miss Roberts threw open the window, tossed the cat outside and made a hissing sound to scare it. She then locked the window and walked over to where the girl still sat on the cement floor.

The woman stared down at her. "If I see that cat in here again, you'll be cleaning toilets for the rest of your days. Do you understand?"

Rose could only nod as tears filled her eyes. She didn't understand why it was wrong to love something as harmless as a kitty cat. She deserved to love something.

"You have six hours now, instead of five. I'll come down when your time is up." The woman slammed the door on her way out. As Ms. Roberts climbed the stairs, Rose could hear her singing "Three Blind Mice" in a high-pitched, off-key voice that made her cringe. "...the farmer's wife who cut off their tails with a carving knife. Three blind mice."

The girl let out a sob as she scrambled to her feet to see where the cat had gone. She stood on her toes again, craning her neck. Suddenly, the cat reappeared.

She opened the window and let him in again. "I'm going to leave the window open so you can come in whenever you want," she whispered.

Over the next few years, she fed and took care of the cat, smuggling crusts of bread and bits of her food down to the basement or leaving them on the windowsill for him. Until she left the orphanage, he was her only friend.

A ringing sound penetrated the air. Rose snapped back to the present. She stuck her hand into her purse, dug out the ringing phone and flipped it open. "Y—yes? Yes, hello?"

"Rose, where are you? For God's sake, you're over an hour late! Why haven't you called?"

"Hi, Rick. Hi. I'm sorry. Really I am. I, uh...I meant to call, but something came up. It looks like I can't come in to work today."

"What do you mean you can't come in to work today? Mr. Halsey's already in from New York. The man's been waiting for the past twenty minutes and you know how he hates to wait. He's a New Yorker, remember?"

With all that was going on this morning, Rose had forgotten Mr. Halsey was flying in to go over his accounts.

"Rose, are you there?"

"Yes. Yes, I'm here."

She couldn't just leave the dogs. They needed her. If her grandmother were here, she wouldn't turn her back on these animals, either. But then again, Rose knew she should not keep Mr. Halsey waiting. He was one of their biggest clients.

The silence over the phone told her Rick was waiting for an explanation and it had better be a good one. Nothing involving dogs, to be sure.

"Block?" he asked again, in a strained voice. "What's going on?"

Rose closed her eyes, willing herself to stay focused. Abandoning the dogs that needed her would be wrong. It would be no different than abandoning children and she knew all too well how that felt. She thought of her father, who left her in the care of an alcoholic mother, who in turn put her in the orphanage. She'd spent three years in that orphanage, trying to understand why her mother abandoned her, before her grandmother won custody of her.

Tears threatened her eyes. Her mother's disappearance

from her life didn't seem that long ago, really. Maybe that's why it still hurt so much.

Rose remembered the Saturday morning when her mother took her into a big brick building, signed some papers, stuffed them into a small blue bag, kissed her on the cheek and said she had groceries to buy. Then her mother drove off in her beat-up Ford and that was the last Rose ever saw of her.

Rose waited day after day for her mother to come back, but she never did. As lonely and sad as it was being in the orphanage, if it wasn't for their care, she might not have survived.

She remembered all too well the pain of being abandoned. How was her pain then any different from the dogs' pain now? Leaving these dogs on the verge of death would only prove that she had learned nothing from her past.

"Rose!" Her boss's voice echoed from the phone in frustration. "Are you, or aren't you coming in?"

She closed her eyes, willing herself again to stay focused. She wished with all her heart that she had the strength to tell Rick the truth, but she couldn't. He would laugh if she told him she had stopped in a rundown neighborhood to help two dogs. She blurted the first lie that came to mind. "I broke my leg, Rick."

The silence on the other end made her wince at what she had said.

"You broke your leg? God, are you all right? How did you break your leg?"

"Well, I didn't really break my leg," she quickly amended. "I just sprained it—badly."

"I see." He paused. "So this means you'll be in when?"

"As soon as I can. My leg's really stiff. I can hardly walk."

He was quiet for a moment, then sighed heavily enough for it to register over the phone. "Tomorrow. I'll reschedule with Halsey for tomorrow at around ten. I'm sure he'll understand."

From the backyard, the German shepherd suddenly barked, making Rose jump from the unexpected show of aggression.

"What was that?"

"A—a dog," was all she could say. She covered the receiver for a moment. She would never have guessed the animal had enough energy to bark so fiercely. The dog could hardly stand.

"I know it's a dog. I also know that you don't have one. You have cats, Rose, and cats don't bark. You didn't go out and get a dog, did you?"

"I—I really have to go, Rick," she insisted, trying not to choke on her words. The sooner she got off the phone the better. She was never a good liar and she hated lying to Rick. He was a good guy, even if he demanded a lot of hours.

"Right. You take care of yourself."

"I will."

"Tomorrow at ten, right?"

"Right. Tomorrow at ten," she repeated, feeling all the more anxious. The dogs. She had to help the dogs. "I really have to go, Rick. Bye."

"It's the first of December and I don't think I have to remind you of what that means around here. Year-end estimates have to go out the door this week."

"I know, Rick. I know. And most of it's already taken care of. I only have a few other things to put together. Look, I really have to go."

"Be here tomorrow at ten."

"Yes, ten. Bye." The conversation ended and all thought of work with it. Rose pushed END, closed the phone case and went back up the alley to check on the dogs.

"Please don't do that!" she scolded the shepherd as the animal began barking again and thrashing about, pulling the chain around its neck tighter. "Your neck will snap. Just stand still, will you? We'll get you out of here when Bob comes. Just—just stay."

The dog barked wildly again, baring its sharp teeth and black gums. Somehow, it wasn't afraid. It was almost as if the dog was communicating with her. The German shepherd was barking as if to say, *When will Bob get here?*

"Soon, soon," she murmured reassuringly, shoving the cell phone into her purse. "And as soon as we can, we'll get you both some food and water."

❧ ❧ Chapter 3

The Dog Rescuers

Finally, Bob's truck appeared and sputtered to a halt, making Rose's heart sputter along with it. Her husband, dressed in faded jeans and a pale blue sweatshirt, stepped out and eyed her. He grimaced and reached into the truck to pull out his green backpack, which he threw over his shoulder.

"Okay, Rose. I'm here, even though it's my first day off in two weeks and I think you're slightly crazy," he said, slamming the truck door behind him.

She nodded and again observed his rough, unshaven features, remembering how once the sight of him had made her quiver. So much had changed.

"You're staring," he said, walking toward her. He paused, keeping a good distance between them and said, "So, where's the dog?"

"Actually, there's two of them."

His eyes snapped to her face. "You didn't say anything about two dogs needing rescuing."

"The other one's the puppy who led me here."

He heatedly slammed his fist into his hand, mouthing what could only be profanity.

"What?" she asked, alarmed. "Is that a problem?"

"Two dogs are a different game. We could have a huge tug of war going on." He sighed, slapping two large hands to his head. "Okay. I can deal with this." He thought for a moment, his hands still pasted to his head, observing her with a combination of annoyance and disdain. "Maybe you should go to work."

Rose stiffened, knowing a battle was about to begin. "I'm not going anywhere. Those dogs need my help, too."

"Those dogs need a chain saw from what you told me on the phone," he firmly stated. "Now go take the fancy suit and heels and scram. I've got work to do." He went around her, still keeping his distance, and headed up the alley to the backyard of the yellow house.

"I'm not going anywhere, Bob," Rose called out, hurrying after him. It really wasn't a matter of pride. She couldn't leave even if she wanted to. The image of that chained dog would haunt her like a ghost.

She found Bob standing at the end of the walkway, his back stiff and his hands in tight fists. She knew just by his stance what he was thinking. They were the same thoughts about these poor animals that pierced her two hours earlier: horror, shame, anger, pain.

Rose slowly made her way toward her husband, her eyes fixed on his taut body, until she was so close she heard his breaths coming in deep uneven gasps.

"Go," he rasped, not turning toward her. "I don't want you around."

"I've spent the last two hours staring at these poor dogs trying to reassure them. I don't want them thinking I abandoned them." Rose squeezed in close to his side, wanting to see the dogs.

A yelp escaped the German shepherd when she came into view. Was the dog about to bite her or was it possible that the dog knew she brought help? She tenderly smiled at the thought. Bob, on the other hand, pulled away from Rose's side.

Rose whispered. "I think she's happy to see me."

"The dog's in pain," he snapped from behind her. "And that can be dangerous for anyone who tries to touch it."

"I don't care if it's dangerous. I'm going to free it." She glanced back at him, wondering what he was thinking. "So are you going to help, or what?"

"Of course I'm going to help. I said I would. I just can't do it now."

"What do you mean, you can't do it now?" Rose hissed, trying not to raise her voice for fear of scaring the dogs. "You have to!"

The German shepherd started yelping again, seemingly pleading along with her.

"Look," he argued, "I'm not equipped. We need some blankets, maybe a cage and a first aid kit. I only brought a dog food container and some water. You don't drag a dog away from its habitat. We have to get it to trust us first."

Digging his hand into his backpack, Bob withdrew a can of dog food. "I bought this at the Seven-Eleven," he said. "Pop open the lid and scoot it as best you can toward the shepherd."

Surprised at his knowledge of handling animals, Rose hesitantly took the can from his hand. "I thought you didn't like animals. How do you know what to do?"

"I had a dog when I was a boy."

She scrutinized him again even more surprised. "You never told me that. I've always thought you hated animals."

He turned away. "He got run over in front of me. It was pretty hard to take for a nine-year-old and I never wanted another one. I don't like to think about it."

She bit her lip and wondered what else she didn't know about this man who seemed to keep so much of his feelings to himself.

He broke in on her thoughts. "The dog's picking up the food's scent and right now that's to our advantage. Go give him some."

She nodded and turned to the dog, while pulling the tab of the can up and open. The popping sound made both of the dogs' ears perk. Rose carefully crept toward the two dogs, now aware that she would have to get closer. From a distance, the dogs were not afraid. But as the space closed between them, fear and trust was becoming an issue. What if the shepherd lunged and bit her?

She paused a few feet away, holding the can before her like an offering to the gods. There were worse things that could happen to her. She could be starving, like this animal. She could be bleeding and near death, as was this animal. All that mattered was the injured dog and the emaciated puppy.

Two pairs of brown eyes stared at her and the can of food. The puppy excitedly sniffed the air and moved out from beneath the larger dog. Rose took another step forward, her legs wobbling from the heels she was wearing. To her disappointment, the puppy barreled backward.

Rose tried not to make eye contact with the German shepherd, although she wanted to. She knew dogs felt threatened when someone looked them in the eye. The air between them was still and tense. One of them was going to snap under the tension. She could feel her heart beating rapidly.

"Okay now. Don't get any closer," a soft voice called from a distance. "Just slide over the food and move back. Real slow."

Rose responded to Bob's voice as if it were her own thoughts and leaned to the side, making sure she didn't drop the can. With one gentle motion, she pushed the dog food across the hard-packed earth of the yard. The can stopped perfectly before the German shepherd. Although the large dog tensed, it didn't react in any other threatened manner.

Relieved, Rose inched back. She'd done it.

She kept her eye on the dogs as she continued to back away. She expected them to tear the can apart between them, but only the pup showed interest in the food. It scrambled forward between the injured legs of the larger dog, began pushing its nose and tongue into the can and gobbled up the food in seconds. When the food was gone, the puppy frantically looked around for more.

Rose was so occupied watching them she backed into something. Or rather, someone. Two strong hands steadied her, only to release her just as quickly. She turned to Bob, who immediately stepped away. "I did it," she murmured.

He only nodded.

"Did you see that? She didn't even bark."

Rose leaned toward him, hoping to get a response. "Well? Are you going to do this?"

He sighed, but gave no other sign of resistance. "Yeah. Only we'll come back tonight when it's dark so no one sees us. You know we're breaking the law, don't you? We're trespassing on private property and soon we'll be stealing someone's animals."

Rose shook her head. "I guess we're partners in this but I don't see it as stealing. We're animal rescuers."

He sighed again and it was not a happy sound.

❖ ❖ Chapter 4

Emergency Measures

"You'd better get to work, Rose. I'll meet you at home tonight and then we'll come back here for the dogs," Bob said as he got into his truck to return to their house. "See you later." He waved as he pulled away.

Rose stood at the curb and watched as Bob drove off. "Maybe someone lives on this block," she murmured when he had gone. "Maybe I can get some more food and water. That'll be my job for today."

She glanced up and down the block to see which house looked like it was being lived in. Then she noticed an elderly woman slowly making her way up toward the stairs of a redbrick house across the street.

Perhaps she could get some food and water from her.

Rose hurried across the street before the woman disappeared into her house.

"Hello? Excuse me!" she called, running up to her. "Ma'am?"

The old woman turned. "What?" she croaked.

Catching her breath, Rose paused at the bottom of the

stairs. "Could you help me? There's a dog that needs help. Two dogs actually."

"Where?" The gray-haired woman looked around. "I don't see any dogs."

"Behind that yellow house over there." Rose pointed to the house across the street. "They badly need water."

"Oh. Is it that shepherd?"

Rose stared at the woman. "You know the dog I'm talking about?"

"Sure, sure." The woman nodded. "I just didn't know the dog was still there. The man who owns that place was arrested maybe a month ago on drug charges. Of course, I wouldn't go on his property. He has some pretty mean looking friends."

Rose choked. "Do you mean to tell me that dog's been back there starving for over a month?"

"I guess." The woman shook her head. "Poor thing. You'd think the guy's sister would have done something. She went through his things after the police took her brother in."

Could people actually live with themselves knowing they left a chained dog to die? "Would it be too much trouble if I asked you for some water for the dogs?" Rose asked.

"Help yourself." The woman shook her head again. "Poor thing. That man never did treat that shepherd good. A lot of people don't treat their dogs good. Come on in. You can get some water."

Rose followed her into the stale-smelling house toward the small kitchen.

The woman pointed to one of the cupboards. "The bowls are up there. Just don't use any of the glass ones. They're the only good dishes I got left."

Nodding, Rose retrieved the largest plastic bowl she could find. Turning the water on in the small kitchen sink, she pushed the bowl under the tap and patiently waited for it to fill.

"Do you want to give the dog something to eat, too?" the woman asked, moving over to the refrigerator. "I have some lunch meat left over. It's not much but I live on a pension, you know."

"Anything. Thank you." Rose turned off the faucet and pulled the filled bowl away from the sink.

"My name's Elspeth," the old woman said, opening the small refrigerator. "And yours?"

"Rose."

"Rose. How did you find out about the dog anyway, Rose?" the woman asked, pulling out a wrapped package with two slices of bologna. "I've been living here all this time and never noticed."

"I was driving by and a little black puppy ran into the road. I followed it to the shepherd. I'm guessing it's the shepherd's puppy."

The woman handed her the bologna. "I thought that dog was a he."

Rose stared at her. Why would a puppy cling to a male German shepherd tied to an oil drum? It didn't make sense. Unless—unless they needed each other that much. It was probably the puppy who was bringing the shepherd food. How else could the dog have survived that long being chained?

"I wish I could do something, but I don't want to get involved. His sister warned everybody not to go over there."

Rose shook her head. "This is fine. Thank you. I have to find a way to get the shepherd off the chain."

"You mean it's still chained?" The old woman shook her head and walked over to a chair. She flopped down in a wobbly manner. "Poor thing. But I'd be careful if I were you. No one from around here would go over there. Even if his sister hadn't come around, we don't go on other folks' property. With his friends, you could get shot," she said.

Rose looked at the old woman's dour face. She obviously wasn't kidding.

"Thank you so much, Elspeth, for this. I'll bring your bowl back later."

Hurrying as best as she could toward the front door without spilling any water, Rose left.

Briskly, she crossed the street and headed back toward

the decrepit yellow house. The closer she got, the more her heart pounded. Feeding the dogs would be the easy part. She and Bob freeing them would be an entirely different matter.

In the backyard of the yellow house again, Rose looked toward the dogs, whose situation hadn't changed. At least she had something for them to eat.

"Hi, guys," she said in a low voice. "I'm back."

She carefully crept toward the dogs, holding out the bologna and the bowl of water. It was only then that she became aware that she would have to get close again to the large shepherd. Much closer.

It was growling now. At a distance she could only feel compassion, but as that safe distance closed between them, fear, as well as rationality, loomed over her. What if the shepherd lunged in desperation this time and bit her?

The shepherd was awfully big, despite his gauntness. A dog that size could snap her arm in half if it wanted to.

Rose paused a few feet away. Holding the food before her, she bolstered her resolve. There were worse things that could happen besides being bitten. All that mattered right now was helping these dogs.

Two pairs of brown eyes stared at her, trying to see what she was holding. The puppy excitedly sniffed the air, moving out from beneath the shepherd.

Rose took another step and almost lost her balance because of her heels. She swayed, spilling some water, but stayed on her feet. Her jerky movements made the puppy barrel back.

She swallowed hard and tried not to make any further eye contact with the dogs. Hopefully they remembered her from this morning. Slowly, she continued stepping forward.

The air between them was tense. She could feel her heart pounding.

When she was as close as she dared get, she leaned down, her fingers gripping the side of the bowl tightly so that water wouldn't spill out, and gently scooted the water toward the shepherd. "Remember me?" she called out softly.

Although the shepherd tensed, it didn't react in any other threatened manner. Rose pulled out the bologna, tore it into small bits and placed it before the dogs in the worn grass. Then she inched back.

Only the puppy showed interest and gulped the little bits of food in seconds. Even in the short time she had been gone, the shepherd looked weaker. He didn't move.

She prayed Bob had meant what he said about coming back that night and hadn't reconsidered. The dogs, especially the shepherd, wouldn't last much longer. No matter what, she had to free these poor animals or she wouldn't be able to live with herself.

Wanting to make the time pass more quickly, Rose decided to go into the office for a few hours. She stopped at a drugstore on the way to get an Ace bandage and wound it around her leg.

Rick looked surprised and embarrassed to see Rose when she showed up at work.

"You didn't have to come in till tomorrow," he said, reddening.

"It's okay," she replied, feigning a limp as she walked to her desk. He didn't know that, because of her lying, she was even more embarrassed than he was.

That afternoon around four she headed home by way of the shortcut through Dalton City. She wanted to make sure the dogs would be all right until she and Bob returned. They looked worn and hungry. The water was gone.

She didn't want to leave the dogs again, but she didn't have much choice. Bob had said they had to try and free them in the darkness.

A low rumble from within made Rose realize she hadn't eaten anything all day. She never ate breakfast and always ate lunch at the office. She glanced at her watch. Almost five. Her stomach rumbled again.

If it weren't for the fact that the shepherd looked like he needed more to eat, she would have waited until she got home. She stood up. There was a McDonald's a few blocks away.

A short while later, Rose came back with a bag full of food. She found the same spot she had earlier rested in and rustled open the bag. The shepherd's ears perked up.

Rose fished out the meat from between the hamburger buns and tossed it over to him. The shepherd bent down his head as best he could, his nose barely touching the ground. He snorted at the food, lifted his head and went back to looking at the wrapper in Rose's hand.

"Aren't you hungry?" Rose asked, concerned. Why wasn't the poor thing eating? Maybe he didn't like hamburgers.

She leaned toward the dog and pulled out the fries. "Maybe you'd like some of these instead?"

She tossed over a few and they landed nearby, somewhere in the grass.

The shepherd leaned down, sniffed the ground and snatched up one of the fries with a chomp. He looked up, saliva dripping from his mouth and stared at the remainder of the fries in her hand.

Rose kept herself from laughing. Whoever heard of a dog that didn't like meat, but loved French fries? She tossed over another handful and watched with a sense of pride as the shepherd picked up each one with the lick of its tongue. The fries were gone within minutes and then the hamburger that had been lying on the ground all this time disappeared, too.

It didn't take long for the little puppy to sniff out that there was more food. He scrambled out toward Rose, his tail wagging and looking for whatever it was his buddy was eating. Rose tossed him a cheeseburger.

He dragged it off to the side, toward the shepherd, ate almost half and then took the rest to the bigger dog. After that, he trotted through the gap in the fence in the back of the yard.

"What are you doing?" a voice asked.

Rose jumped and looked toward the alley where a small boy stood, holding a bowl. Wasn't he supposed to be at school? No. Of course not. School was out hours ago. With her girls in college, Rose almost forgot how that whole grade school thing worked.

"I'm feeding them," she said.

"My Grandma told me to come over. She saw your car."

"Your grandmother?"

"Her name's Elspeth Baker. We live in that house over there. She said she gave you some food for the dogs this morning. She asked me to bring this." He held up the bowl of cereal he was carrying. "It's not much, but—"

"That's really nice of your grandmother. They need plenty of food, that's for sure." She waved toward the dogs.

The dark-haired boy nodded and walked toward her. "You're the lady Grandma said came over asking for food and water earlier today, right?" he asked, pausing when he was within a few feet of the dogs.

She smiled. "Yes. Elspeth didn't say she had a grandson."

"No one calls her Elspeth. They just call her Grandma."

"Of course." She couldn't help widening her grin. He was awfully cute. He reminded her of her daughter Margaret when she was little. Serious and to the point.

To her surprise, the young boy suddenly walked up to the German shepherd and squatted, his face only a few inches away from the large dog. He placed the bowl of cereal on the ground, got up and walked back to where Rose sat.

"Have you done that before?" she asked, in awe of what he had just done.

"Done what?" He looked at her as if she were strange.

"Walk right up to him."

He shrugged. "I'm not scared of dogs."

"I should say not. Have you given him food before?"

He shook his head. "I didn't know he was back here. Grandma tells me not to go on other people's property. Though, if I heard him barking, I would have helped him. I just never heard him." He paused. "Are you gonna save him?"

She nodded. "I hope so."

"Why?"

"Because he's suffering." She smiled. "I'm going home to get my husband. Then we're coming back so he can cut the dog loose."

"And then what?"

"And then we'll take him to the emergency clinic so we can make him better."

"Oh." He shoved his hands into his pockets and looked back at the dog. "You need help?"

Rose observed him for a moment. If Bob didn't come back, maybe she could get this boy to help her. "What's your name?"

"Mike."

"Well, Mike, it's nice to meet you. My name's Rose."

He nodded. "There are more dogs like this around here, you know. A lot of strays that are starving. Just like this one. I see 'em all the time." He waved toward the front of the house. "They go through garbage cans looking for food all the time. People put rocks on the cans' lids to keep the dogs away, but that don't stop 'em. They're hungry, you know."

"And do you help them?"

"I try. But Grandma says there ain't enough food in our fridge to feed them and we gotta eat, too. Grandma's too old to work and I'm only ten." He scratched his head and walked toward the alley. "Well, I gotta go. I told Grandma I'd be right back after I fed the dog."

"Sure, sure."

"If you need me, just come on over. Well, bye." He held up a hand and disappeared.

At least some help was being offered. Although how much help could a ten-year-old be? She sighed and went back to looking at the shepherd.

"I'm going home to get Bob," she said. "I'll only be gone a short while and then I'll be back to get you."

She wondered if the dog understood. Its eyes were closed and it was moaning piteously.

Chance for Survival

"No," her husband firmly said, shaking his head. "I've been thinking about it and it's too dangerous for us to go get those mutts from southeast Dalton City."

Rose stared at Bob, who lay on the couch flipping through different channels on the television set. "Bob, please. I don't know what else to do."

He clicked off the television, clearly agitated, and sat up. "I came when you called this morning. I've been on the road for two damn weeks. Two weeks. Give me a break, will you? Call a veterinarian. I'm sure they deal with this stuff all the time. Just make sure it doesn't cost us much. We've got girls in college, remember?"

Rose threw her hands up in the air in frustration. "I don't know why I'm even married to you! You're gone all the damn time and when I do ask you to do something which means a lot to me, you say yes, raising my hopes, and then change your mind, dashing them. Bob, for God's sake, that shepherd is bleeding to death as we speak! We have to do something."

"I'm not going into that neighborhood again for a dog that isn't mine," he insisted. "I'm a truck driver who has a company to look after, remember? I'm not a police officer or a dog catcher."

Rose stormed out of the room. Only now did she realize why she worked so much, never missing a day even when she was sick.

It was because she feared being confronted with the bitter loneliness that seemed to follow her all her life. The sort of loneliness and suffering that was similar to being chained to a fifty-five-gallon oil drum in a yard strewn with trash. The sort of loneliness and neglect a woman felt after one failed marriage, only to end up in one in which her husband was never home. The sort of loneliness a woman felt when her two daughters, the only love she could ever count on and whom she raised practically on her own, left her and went away to college.

She yanked up the kitchen phone and began dialing the veterinarian she used for her two cats. Then she pushed the cut-off button. What could her vet do? Was he going to leave his clinic and personally saw off the dog's chain on someone's private property? Of course not.

But who else would take her seriously? "Maybe I should call nine-one-one," she murmured. As far as she was concerned, it was an emergency.

She dialed the police station.

A female voice responded, "This is police headquarters. Is this an emergency?"

"I need a policeman down in southeast Dalton City, between Kenneth and Bell. I'd give you an address, but I didn't see one coming in. It's the only yellow house in the neighborhood, though. The rest are made of brick."

"What is this concerning, Miss?"

"A dog. There's a dog that really needs help. It's chained to an oil drum and its shoulder is cut to the bone. I think the bone is broken, it's bleeding and—"

"Is the dog dead?"

Why did everybody she call for help ask her that? "No, the dog is not dead!"

"I'm sorry, but we only take people calls."

"What do you mean, people calls!" she exclaimed. "I'm a person and I'm calling, aren't I? I need someone to come out and help me help this dog! It's been out there a long time and—"

"I'm sorry, but we don't take calls like this, Miss."

"What kind of calls do you take? This is an emergency! And an emergency is an emergency."

"I'm sorry, I can't help you," the dispatcher said. "Call Animal Life. They take care of that sort of thing. The number is five-five-five, six-one-eight-nine."

"I already called them and they say they can't go on somebody's property. Couldn't you just send a policeman over to see what's going on? I mean, from what one of the neighbors told me, the police arrested the dog's owner on drug charges. You should at least take responsibility for the dog."

"Miss, we just don't handle animal rescues. You'd best call Animal Life. Did you get that number? Five-five-five, six-one-eight-nine."

Rose took it down with a shaky hand. "Please, if you could just get an officer to meet me, I—"

"Call Animal Life. They'll help you." The line clicked off.

Tears overwhelmed her. She didn't understand why it was so hard for everyone to see that she needed help. The dog was going to bleed to death, she was sure.

Rose had no choice but to make the call. She only hoped this time she'd be able to convince them to help her. She repeated the number out loud and dialed it just as fast.

"Animal Life. This is James."

Rose swallowed back her tears, trying to find her voice. "Hi. I—I was hoping you could help me. I really need your help."

"Sure. With what?"

She sniffed and took in a shaky breath. "I found a dog in Dalton City that needs immediate medical attention. Someone cut his shoulder pretty bad and—"

"I'm so sorry, Ma'am. We just can't help you."

Rose ran her hand over her forehead in misery.

"We're not currently staffed for such cases. Even if we could come out and pick up the dog, more than likely, if it's in bad shape, we'd have to put it down."

"Put it down?" she asked, alarmed. "Why?"

"As far as treatments go, we don't have the budget to treat every dog that comes through the door. That's just how it is. I'm sorry."

Rose shook her head, fighting off a sob. Why didn't anyone want to help her? Here she was trying so hard to help this poor dog and people who were paid to save animals weren't even doing their jobs. The irony of that realization struck her painfully for the second time that day.

"Listen to me," Rose muttered, her words heavy and filled with pain. "I don't know who to turn to. My husband won't help me, the police won't help me, even the Humane Society won't help me. You have to help me. Please."

"I wish I could, but I can't," the man insisted. "But maybe I can try to find someone who can. What's your number?"

She gave it to him.

"Got it. I'll have someone call you."

"When?" she insisted, looking at the clock on the kitchen wall. It was already eight. She had left the dog alone for almost three hours. "This dog doesn't have much time. When?"

"As soon as I can."

"All right."

"Hold on."

"Sure, I can. It's the dog who can't." Rose hung up the phone and hit the wall with the palm of her hand. It was bad enough she had left the two dogs alone again. With each passing moment, the shepherd had less of a chance of surviving.

She would wait one hour and if no one called in that time, she was going out to Bob's toolshed to get the chain saw. If she had to saw the chain off the dog herself, then that's what she'd do.

An hour and fifteen minutes later, Rose lifted her head

from the kitchen table and stared for the umpteenth time at the clock. Still no call. She closed her eyes, her head aching. She couldn't wait any longer.

Although she hadn't seen the dogs for over three hours, the image of the shepherd with its gaping wound, its thin neck tightly chained to an oil drum, moaning in its sleep, and a baby, a tiny puppy bony from hunger, lying in the bigger dog's puddle of blood, still scorched her thoughts.

"Rose?"

Opening her eyes, she looked toward the doorway where her husband stood still dressed in jeans and a sweatshirt. He still hadn't shaved and his blond hair stood on end as if he had just woken up. He approached her, then moved to the other side of the table, pulled out a chair and sat down across from her. She met his penetrating blue eyes.

"Listen to me, Rose. We've been married how long? Almost ten years?"

She nodded.

He sighed. "In the years we've been together, you know what I've noticed most about you?" He brought a finger to his forehead and pointed at his head. "That you don't think with this all the time." He then brought that same finger to the center of his chest and rested it there. "Most of the time, you think with this. And that's the difference between you and me. You get all wrapped up with the way you feel, while I get wrapped up with the way I think."

Rose stared at the finger that rested on his chest. He was right. In her nearly forty years, she had done nothing but dwell on her heart.

And how many times had her heart misled her? She sighed. Too many times. It had misled her when she was a ten-year-old child to believe her mother would some day come back into her life. Her mother never did.

If she had used her head instead of her heart, she would have told herself the truth. Alcoholics, after all, could never commit to anything. They were committed to the bottle.

If she had used her head, she wouldn't have suffered so much. It was again her heart, after all, that had misled her to marry her ex-husband and to live with him through the endless drinking and the disgusting parade of women. At least that marriage had produced two wonderful daughters.

Still, she always regretted that she and Bob had not had children of their own. She knew deep inside him he regretted it, too, even though he enjoyed being part of raising Margaret and Emily.

Whatever part he was there for, that is. She often wondered why she had to fall in love with a man whose small company hauled cargo for long distances. He was a truck driver married more to the road and the other drivers he now employed, than to her.

"Do you still want me to help you?" he finally asked, dropping his hand down to his side.

"Yes," she whispered. "Are you going to?"

He nodded. "Just this once. You hear? I don't want you getting all wrapped up in things like this that are dangerous and against the law. What people do with their animals is their business. I'm not saying it's right, but there's no way in hell you can help every damn abused animal that comes along. And don't give me that look," he warned her, wagging a finger at her. "I'm just laying things out the way they are. I'll help you with these two dogs if you promise me here and now that that's it. I mean, how the hell did you find these pitiful creatures anyway?"

Rose stood up and snatched the keys from the kitchen counter. "Would you believe me if I said they found me? 'Pitiful creatures' have always come to me. Maybe because they know that I was once a pitiful creature, too. A pitiful creature that would understand them."

She paused at the back door. "Which one of your saws can cut through a thick chain?"

Bob stood and came toward her, a determined look on his face. "Rose, I said I'm coming. I'll bring bolt cutters. You get some blankets." He threw open the door, almost banging it against her, and strode into the backyard.

Rose hurried after him into the garage he had already opened. "You don't have to help me, you know," she pointed out, watching him pick up a few different saws.

He grabbed a towel and wrapped them tightly. Picking up a large bag, he shoved the towel-wrapped tools inside. "I'm trying to reach out here," he snapped. "You always tell me how I don't reach out enough. You always tell me that I'm not around to help you. So I'm helping you, damn it. Let's go. We'll take your car. Toss me the keys." He opened the door to the van. "Get in."

Rose scrambled inside. "Thanks, Bob."

"Yeah. Thank me after we get the dogs," he muttered. "We might not be able to get them, you know. We could get arrested or worse."

"We'll get them. Don't you worry. We'll get them."

Without another word, the drive to southeast Dalton City began. The silence continued until they got to the block with the yellow house.

❖ ❖ Chapter 6

A Form of Lunacy

Bob parked the vehicle on a side street and looked around at the dilapidated buildings, shaking his head. "All we need is for the van to get stolen."

Rose impatiently tapped the dashboard and looked at the lighted clock display. "It's after nine, Bob," she murmured. "Let's go."

She took in a shaky breath. Only one out of several streetlamps lit the dark and quiet street, giving the area a sinister feel. She took another deep breath, trying to release some of the tension that was building within her. She never did anything crazy like this. Then again, was saving a dog considered crazy? Of course not! Not unless compassion was a form of lunacy.

She stared out at the desolate street with its unevenly parked cars and felt her stomach cramping. All she could hear was the staccato intake of her breath and her husband's steady breathing beside her.

"Are you ready?" he finally asked, getting out of the van

and coming around to her side. She sat there transfixed for a few moments.

Bob waved a flashlight beneath his chin, highlighting his unshaven face. "Rose, we better do this now. Hurry up."

Rose took in a deep breath and scrambled to open the door, her heart still pounding. "I'm sorry," she muttered, getting out of the van.

Bob clicked the flashlight off and stepped away. "Sorry won't cut it if someone catches us, you know."

Rose wiped her wet palms into her sweat pants.

"Let's just do this."

"Don't make any noise and follow me."

Rose nodded and trailed after his shadowy figure, anxiously looking around to make sure no one was watching. Despite the dogs being abandoned, she felt nervous going back to a drug dealer's property, especially at night. Her throat went dry as they walked down the street, turned the corner and went through the dark passageway, bringing her closer to the dogs she couldn't push from her mind. Her stomach growled. She had forgotten to eat again.

"Now, I want you to take the flashlight," Bob whispered, holding it out to her. "Shine it to the side when I tell you to and don't aim it at the dogs. It might confuse them."

Rose took the light and looked toward the shadows of the yard, her eyes searching for the oil drum. A low whimper told her where the German shepherd was. "We're here, sweetie," she gently cooed into the darkness. The whimper lulled and there was a slight rustle in the grass.

Biting her lip, Rose watched Bob slide the bag from his shoulder. She had never seen this side of him. Where did it come from? Duty? Compassion? Or something much deeper that was equally primitive and protective?

"Turn it on."

"Oh, right." She fumbled with the flashlight, trying to find the switch. As she clicked it on, the darkness around her retreated into the corners of the yard. She was surprised to see Bob already beside the two dogs, equipped with a saw. She was even more surprised to find the two dogs watching Bob with what she could only describe as admiration. The massive German shepherd leaned toward him.

Bob stepped sideways toward the dented oil drum and gently motioned Rose to approach.

There was a silent trust being communicated among all of them and if that trust was going to continue, she would have to set aside the fear of being attacked. She stepped forward and kept doing so until she stood next to Bob.

"Shine the flashlight right here on the chain," he instructed.

Lifting a shaky arm, she did as she was asked, illuminating the rusty rings of iron.

Bob examined them, drawing closer to the German shepherd. Although the puppy had lost its courage and scampered away beneath the larger dog, the German shepherd stood there patiently, its shoulder still bleeding as Bob tried to free him.

"The bastard didn't even put a collar on him," Bob commented, lifting his head to look at Rose. "He just wrapped the chain around the base of the dog's neck, put a lock at the end of it and left the animal here to die."

Rose swallowed hard.

"For all we know, that puppy over there saved this shepherd by bringing him food. It would certainly explain how he survived this long."

"God, Bob. Can we free him?"

"I'm going to try." He began cutting at one of the links farthest from the shepherd.

Rose couldn't help staring at the large dog as the sound of screeching metal resounded around them. Large brown eyes met hers in the darkness and held her gaze. That gaze was so powerful and so full of life, Rose almost burst into tears. Who could do such a thing? Who could take a life, be it in the form of an animal or a human, and treat it with such cruelty?

Bob finally stopped cutting and the chain fell loose. He leaned toward the shepherd and tenderly unwound the remainder of the chain without any resistance. "He's free."

The shepherd stood motionless, seeming unsure what to do now that he had been liberated. The puppy watched them intently.

"He's free," Rose repeated, stepping toward the dogs. "Now we have to get to the animal hospital."

"I'll carry him to the car and then we can wrap him in blankets."

Rose looked at the shepherd, who was still frozen in place, and wondered whether he would even allow himself to be lifted. "Do you think he'll—"

"If he let me undo the chain, he'll let me carry him." Bob motioned over to the left. "Go get the puppy."

She nodded and moved toward the small dog sitting a few feet away. Before the puppy could scamper off, she scooped him up. Warm fur and kicking legs greeted her and she happily brought the creature close to her chest.

Bob had a much harder task lifting such an enormous creature, but the shepherd licked Bob who grunted as he shifted the dog in his arms and strode out of the yard at a surprisingly fast rate.

Rose hurried after him. "I can't believe how big he is," she commented. "His head is about the size of a cow's head."

"Yeah." Bob grunted again. "And just imagine if he were properly fed. I'm carrying only the mass of his fur and bones, you know."

"Let's put him in the backseat with the puppy. I'm sure they'd be happier together anyway."

"He's filthy and he probably has fleas, too."

"The van will be just fine. I'm worried about the dog, not the backseat. Let me go open the door for you." She hurried ahead of him and unlocked the back door, still holding the lively puppy against her chest.

Bob staggered toward the car and, lowering himself as best he could, gently placed the dog on the rear seat. Once the shepherd was safely inside, Bob sighed and observed Rose in the dim light of the street.

The puppy's paws dug into Rose's chest just as she noticed Bob's gaze. Suddenly, she felt nervous. But why should she be nervous? This was Bob. "What?" was all she could say as he continued to stare at her.

"All I have to say is that you're not like any woman I've ever met. Even after all these years, you're still full of surprises."

"I could say the same for you."

Rose quickly handed him the puppy. Now was not a good time for conversation.

"I'll take that as a compliment," he said. "Now let's get these two some help."

"Right."

Rose never knew how fast Bob could drive until they had a yelping puppy and a bleeding German shepherd in the backseat. There was no more conversation, which was fine with Rose who, at that moment, preferred silence. Besides, she knew Bob needed to concentrate on the road. They needed to get to the vet and do the one thing she had been pining to do all morning and afternoon—save the shepherd.

After twenty minutes or so, the clinic appeared. Bob hooked a quick right and pulled the van into the parking lot, taking the space closest to the door.

Rose jumped out of the van. "Wait here," she called to him. "I'll be right back."

"Hey, what about the dogs?"

"I'm going in to get help," she told him before she closed the door. "I don't want you having to carry the shepherd again."

Once inside the clinic, help appeared in the form of two burly young men—veterinary technicians who assisted the doctors. They followed Rose out into the parking lot and carefully lifted the German shepherd from her van. Together, the two men carried the animal into the clinic, with Rose and Bob trailing behind.

Inside, Rose worriedly watched as the two assistants strapped the German shepherd onto a cart. She hated the fact that the dog had to endure restraints similar to the chain that had enslaved him just a few minutes ago. After a few growls from the dog, they tied a muzzle over his mouth.

"I don't know if we should be restraining him like this," she finally said to one of the men. "He's been through a lot."

"Don't worry," he assured her, adjusting the muzzle. "This is normal procedure. It'd be very hard to administer any form of treatment with him moving or biting."

"He wouldn't bite," Rose said defensively as Bob handed the puppy to the other veterinary technician.

"We can't take any chances," the man responded.

"We'll take it from here," the other quickly added, holding the puppy close to his chest. "Just fill out the rest of the paperwork and we'll see you in a few days. The puppy should be fine, but this one here's going to need surgery. He's in bad shape."

A few days? How could she possibly wait that long without knowing whether the shepherd was going to be all right?

As she watched the young men roll away the large dog, she fought the urge to cry. It didn't feel right to her. It was as if she had rescued him only to let others tie him down again.

"Wait!" She hurried toward them and moved around the two men. She couldn't let the shepherd go without comforting him.

She leaned over the cart and rested a hand on his head. His eyes, his large, trusting eyes, stared back and a tearful smile came to her face. "It'll be all right," she gently whispered. "You're going to be just fine. I promise."

She rubbed his forehead again, savoring the feel of his fur. A crust of caked dirt crumbled away with each stroke. When was the last time he had a bath? Had he ever even had one?

The shepherd licked her hand and closed his eyes.

"Make sure you give him a bath," she insisted.

"Don't you worry about that," the dark-haired assistant said, half-smiling. "We'll pamper him in every possible way."

"Good. And—" An arm took hold of Rose and pulled her away before she could finish giving more instructions.

"Let them do their thing," Bob urged.

She nodded and watched the shepherd and the puppy disappear through the double doors, leaving her and Bob in the waiting area. Rose paced the floor and vowed with each frantic step that she would give everything she ever owned to make sure those two dogs would be all right. A tight squeeze of her arm reminded her that Bob was still with her.

"Everything's going to be just fine, Rose."

"I hope so." She tried not to notice how strong Bob's hand was, pressing into her skin. She couldn't remember the last time he had touched her with such genuine feeling.

He took his hand away after a few moments and looked toward the front desk. "There's some more paperwork to fill out. Do you want to do it?"

She nodded.

"I'll be in the car." He put up a hand and headed toward the double glass doors at the entrance.

Rose turned to the receptionist to finish filling out the papers. She picked up the pen from the counter and wrote down all the numbers where she could be reached. "Have them call me as soon as they know anything."

The woman nodded and took up the papers. "Have a good night."

Rose shook her head. A good night would have been knowing whether the two dogs she and Bob had rescued were going to live. She knew she wasn't going to be able to sleep until she learned their fate.

❧ ❧ **Chapter 7**

Nightmares

When Rose woke the next morning, she stretched then followed her cat Peaches into the kitchen, yawning. Her mind was still hazy. All night she had dreamed about dogs. Hundreds and hundreds of dogs trapped in cages. She could still hear them all simultaneously barking, like a chorus of misfortune. It was no wonder she had such a severe headache.

"Meow."

"Yes, I know you're hungry, Peaches. Where's Scooter?" She stifled another yawn. "So what will it be this morning? Dried slop or wet slop?"

"Meow."

"Wet slop it is." She grabbed a can of cat food and pulled the lid open.

She glanced at the clock just as she was bending down, and froze. "No. No, it can't be. Ten o'clock?" Her boss was going to kill her! Bob had left early and hadn't reset the alarm clock.

"Darn it," she grumbled.

She dumped half the contents of the can in one bowl, the other half in a second bowl and threw the empty tin into the sink. "Of all days," she muttered.

She headed for the bathroom, grabbed a brush and yanked it through her hair. Hurriedly, she glanced at herself in the mirror.

"Rubber band. I need a rubber band." She pulled open a drawer, pushing aside lotions and tampons. "Rubber band. Where's the rubber band?" She slammed the door shut and began searching the others, but still no rubber band. Not knowing what else to do, she let her hair hang loose.

"Meow."

She jumped over her other cat, Scooter, and sprinted toward the bedroom. Pulling on the first dress she saw, she walked back to the bathroom, blue skirt halfway over her head. She hit the frame of the doorway.

"Oww!" She pulled the dress down and rubbed her head. She could tell it was not going to be a good day.

Rose paused when she got to the kitchen and suddenly remembered she was going to be driving through Dalton City on her way to work. She never thought of throwing food out the window on her way to work before, but why not? Elspeth's grandson, Mike, told her there were other hungry dogs in the area.

She looked back at the clock. She was already late. What were a few more minutes? She opened the refrigerator and grabbed some cold cuts and cheese. She'd go shopping for some dog food later. At least that way, she would feel like she was doing something and that some other poor dog wouldn't go hungry.

Somehow, she finished getting ready and left.

"You're late," Rick snapped, coming toward her as she arrived in the office.

"I know, I know," Rose apologized, balancing the stack of folders she had brought with her.

"Lucky for you Mr. Halsey is still around." He took some of the folders from her. "How's your leg?"

"My leg?" She blinked, then reddened remembering the

fib she had told him when she was late yesterday and realizing she had forgotten to put the bandage back on. "It's fine. Just fine."

"Yeah, it looks fine. You're not even limping. Come on. Let's get this over and done with."

They walked past Lillian, the receptionist, who had just picked up the phone.

"Yes, please hold. Rose?" Lillian put out red manicured nails to get her attention. "There's a call for you."

"She's not taking any calls right now, Lillian," Rick said firmly as he continued heading toward the conference room.

"It's some animal clinic. Are your cats sick or something?" Lillian asked. "It sounds urgent."

Rose almost dropped the folders she was holding. The attendant at the clinic said they would call her in a few days. Why were they calling now? "I'll take it," she said, plopping everything she was holding onto Lillian's desk and holding out her hand.

"Rose, take a message. Mr. Halsey's waiting," her boss sharply reminded her.

"This will only take a moment." She took the phone. "Hello?"

"Rose? Rose Block?"

"Yes. This is Rose Block."

"Hi, I'm Doctor Winston from the Hayley Clinic. You dropped off two dogs last night. Is that right?"

"Yes." She nodded anxiously. Bob didn't know it, but she was prepared to pay any amount of money it took to nurse the shepherd and the puppy back to health. "How are they?"

There was a pause. "The uh...the German shepherd you brought in last night died this morning during surgery. He didn't respond well to the anesthetic and there was nothing we could do to revive him. I'm sorry. We did everything we could."

Rose stared at the folders on the desk before her in disbelief and blinked to keep her eyes clear from of the tears that were forming.

No. She hadn't heard right. "He couldn't possibly have died."

"He had every ailment a dog could possibly have. A broken shoulder, mange, cellulitus on all four legs, heartworm, fleas, even a form of kennel cough."

"I—I don't understand," she whispered, her knees beginning to falter. "All those things sound treatable. I mean—"

"Mrs. Block, I can tell you're upset. Why don't you come in and we'll talk?"

"Yes, maybe that would be best. I have a meeting, but I can be there in an hour or so," she murmured.

How she got through the meeting without completely breaking down she wasn't sure. Rick, noticing her condition, blamed it on the supposed accident from the previous day and let her go as soon as he could, although he didn't look happy about it. He followed her out to the reception desk.

"Rose, what's going on?" he asked, trying to take hold of her shoulders.

"The German shepherd died," she sobbed, finally breaking down. "He died."

"You had a German shepherd?"

She shook her head. "I found him. I—I found him and I tried to save him and I couldn't. I—I couldn't."

Her boss stared at her. "It's not your dog? Why are you crying?"

"Because he died!" She turned away from him, choking on her tears, wishing she could have done something different. It was her fault, after all. She should never have left the dog chained to that oil drum for the rest of the afternoon. Those few hours proved to be as precious as his life.

A hand touched her back. "Rose, I'm sorry," Rick softly said. "That sounded bad. I didn't mean it to come out the way it did."

"I'm so sorry, too," Lillian whispered, coming around the desk to comfort her.

"I—I just can't believe he died," Rose whispered, moving away from them. Was it because she and Bob waited till nightfall to go back?

"Oh God!" she wailed, tears streaming down her face.

"The dog's last moments were spent strapped against a—a metal cart! I could have done something. Instead, he died alone in a clinic after being deprived of everything a living creature has a right to."

"Rose, you're falling apart. Maybe we should—"

"I can't believe he died." She wanted the pain inside her head and inside her heart to go away, but knew this was only the beginning.

It took all her strength to drive to the clinic. She had trusted them to save the shepherd. If she had any doubts, she would never have left the clinic last night. If she had any doubts, she would have taken the shepherd elsewhere. If she had any doubts, she might have saved his life.

"No," she said, refusing to accept what the doctor had told her. "He shouldn't have died. He lived through everything else. Why would he just die?"

She pulled over to the side of the road and turned off the motor, feeling the hysteria inside her building until she couldn't take it anymore. She buried her face in her hands and wept. Each sob brought more pain ringing in her chest and mind like death knells. She had tried so hard to save him. So hard.

She pulled out her cell phone and tapped the numbers she rarely used—Bob's cell phone when he was on the road. She pressed SEND and waited for him to answer.

"Yeah? This is Block." The phone crackled.

"He died, Bob," she yelled at him. "He died!"

"Rose? Is that you?" The phone crackled again. "Is something wrong? Why are you calling me on the road?"

"Because the shepherd died," she said tearfully. She tried to get hold of herself, but couldn't.

"Are you at work?" he asked. "Maybe you should go home."

Rose shook her head, wiping away her tears. Why was it no one seemed to understand what she was feeling? "I'm not going home. I'm going to the clinic." She hung up and sat there a few moments, tears running down her cheeks.

Long minutes passed before she was able to finish the drive. Pulling up to the clinic, she was shocked to see

Bob's truck parked in front. She hurried inside, wondering why he came.

The receptionist recognized her and gave a subdued wave. Bob was with the vet in the reception area. "I'm sorry he didn't make it," the vet was saying. "His heart was just too weak from malnutrition, not to mention eaten up by worms. And overall, the wound to his leg was so infected we would've had to amputate it. Even the chain around his neck caused a bad form of gangrene. Really, it was for the better. He's not in pain anymore. The puppy, on the other hand, is just fine. We'll keep him for a few days, at no extra cost, just to be sure."

For Rose, hearing the details about the shepherd was devastating. She stood before the veterinarian feeling weak and nauseous.

"Thank you," Bob said, shaking the man's hand. "Thank you for all your efforts."

The vet nodded and walked out, leaving them alone.

Rose buried her face in her hands and wept again. "I should have tried harder. I should have done more."

Bob's firm hand rested on her back. "We did everything we could, Rose. I wish we could have saved him, but, believe me, I learned years ago, sometimes there's nothing you can do."

She rested against Bob for a moment, hating herself. "That shepherd, that same precious dog that stared at me with conviction that I would save him, is dead. And what sort of a life did it live? It didn't even get a meal! We should have kept this from happening!" she cried. "Why did we wait? Maybe if we'd taken him the first time—"

"Rose, what we did was against the law. You just can't—"

"All we did was come back with a saw and free a suffering animal. I should have stayed with him until that night. I should have stayed at the clinic. Instead, he died alone after living under horrendous conditions!"

"He wasn't alone. There were compassionate people and other animals here. And he was warm and cared for. That's a lot more than he had before."

"But he died!" she lashed out. She wanted the all-encompassing pain she was feeling to go away. "He died! He died! I let him die!"

Bob reached out his hand and took hold of her shoulder. "Please, don't do this to yourself."

"But he died alone and scared and—"

"I can guarantee you that for the first time in his life he felt loved," he said, leaning toward her. "I know it. The way he laid his head on my shoulder when I carried him to the car told me he felt loved."

She wept even harder. "If we didn't wait, he wouldn't have died," she sobbed. "If we had just done it there and then none of this would have happened."

"Now, you don't know that, Rose."

"But I feel that way! I blame myself," she said pointing to herself, "and I blame you," she added, pointing at him. "And I blame every jerk that wouldn't help me yesterday morning when I tried to save him!"

Bob shook his head and stepped away. "I want you to go home and get some rest."

"I have to pay the bill."

"I'll pay the bill." He reached into his back pocket for his wallet. "You go."

"No, you go! I'm paying the bill!" Rose walked over to the receptionist, pulled out her wallet and plopped it on the counter. "How much do I owe?" she asked the woman.

"Let me calculate the total. It'll just be a moment, Ma'am."

Waiting for the bill while listening to the shuffle of paper and the tapping of keys on the calculator made Rose want to scream. She couldn't stand there much longer. All she thought about was the shepherd dying. How was she going to live with herself knowing that she could have done more, should have done more? She hadn't even had a chance to name him. He died without a name.

"Five hundred dollars," the woman finally said.

"Five hundred dollars!" Bob cried, coming up to them. "We brought in a puppy and a shepherd, not two elephants!"

"Bob, for heaven's sake, stop it!" Rose yelled at him,

wishing he would just leave. "They tried to save his life, didn't they? It doesn't matter how much it is. It just doesn't matter." She handed a credit card to the receptionist.

Bob grabbed Rose's arm and turned her toward him. "You're going to pay five hundred dollars for a dog that isn't even yours? Are you crazy?"

"Yes," she coldly replied. "Now let go of me. Perhaps if you had helped me sooner, none of this would have happened."

His brows sharpened. "You're not blaming me for all of this now, are you?"

"You and everyone else." She freed herself from his possessive grasp and picked up a pen to sign the credit card receipt. She then thought of something else and said to the receptionist, "What about burial arrangements?"

The woman stared at her as if she didn't understand.

"The dog died," Rose stated. "You don't just throw the body in a garbage can, do you?"

"Well, no. No, of course not," the woman quietly said, standing up. She reached into an overhead filing cabinet for some papers and then handed them to Rose. "Here. Sign these. They're release forms. We'll put the dog in a body bag for you, so you can make your own arrangements."

"Thank you." Rose hurriedly signed her name and shoved the papers back at the woman. "Where do I pick him up?" she asked, her lip quivering.

"The back door," the woman replied.

"Thank you," Rose whispered.

"Rose, I have to get back on the road," Bob said. "I have to finish this delivery. You know I'll be gone a few days and I really think—"

She interrupted him. "Go. You're always gone anyway."

"Hey, I'm sorry."

Rose snatched up her half of the receipt and her credit card and turned to leave. She couldn't deal with Bob. How could he think about work at a time like this?

"What about the puppy?" Bob asked. "Are you gonna just leave him?"

She turned back to face him and wiped away tears that

were still falling. "The vet said he'd keep him for a few days at no extra cost. I'll pick him up then. You don't have to do anything else. Just go."

"I came out to help you, didn't I? I didn't have to help. I didn't have to do a damn thing you know!" He strode out.

Rose's lip quivered. "I . . . I have to go," she choked, turning away from the stare of the receptionist.

As she ran out into the parking lot, Rose knew that if she was ever going to make sense of her life again, ever feel better than she did right then, she would have to do something to alleviate the suffering of creatures who were being abused. Though she didn't know how or what, she knew she had to do something.

❖ ❖ Chapter 8

The Smell of Death

A snow shower had begun gently falling as the red-haired man questioningly held out a sagging, gray body bag. "Do you want me to put him in the back?" he asked.

Rose tried to swallow her emotions as she scrambled to open the van's side door. "No. Just—just lay him in the backseat."

He raised an inquisitive brow, but was silent. He hauled the heavy body bag onto the seat, then pushed it all the way inside. He stepped back and closed the side door of the van.

"I'm sorry about your dog, Ma'am."

"Yes, me too." Blinded by tears, she opened the car door and got in.

No sooner had she closed the door than the smell of death filled her nostrils. She gagged, covered her mouth with a shaky hand and reached out with her other hand to hit the window button. She had to get home before she felt any sicker.

She peeled out of the parking lot and dodged a car that crossed her path. Tears streamed down her face as she clutched the steering wheel trying to stay in control.

As she drove down the street, she rigidly rotated the wheel, making the turn onto the highway. The sound of weighted plastic shifted in the backseat and Rose felt her stomach shift along with it.

She reached out and clicked on the radio, trying not to think about the shepherd lying a few feet behind her. Classical music enveloped her, flutes floating, piano keys tickling and muted timpani rolling. But instead of soothing her, as classical music usually did, now it only agitated her.

She hit the button for another station.

Hard rock shook the panels of her car, the electric guitars screaming, drums thundering, killing whatever it was the musicians wanted dead. She turned the volume up, way up, trying to drown out her thoughts.

Finally, she reached the house.

Silencing the radio that had blasted for the past few miles, Rose pulled the key out of the ignition. She sat there for a few moments, rubbing her swollen eyelids.

She stepped out of the car and for the first time since she left the clinic, looked into the backseat. There he was, inside that light gray bag, waiting. Except there was no end to his waiting. How she prayed that for his sake there was a heaven for animals. To suffer and to die without there being anything else seemed unthinkable.

She sniffed and opened the back door. Just don't think about it, she told herself. Don't think about it. Just do it.

She took in a deep breath, wrapped her arms around the end of the bag and pulled. The bag shifted but only slightly. He was a lot heavier than she thought. She yanked harder until the bag finally slid out, swiftly dropping to the ground with a thud.

"Oh God," she whispered, bending over to try to pick up the heavy bag. Somehow she awkwardly managed to get the bag off the ground. Although she felt new tears threatening, she willed herself to stay focused. She knew if she started crying again, she wouldn't have the strength to carry him into the backyard.

She staggered up the sidewalk and moved toward her backyard. The gate to her yard was open, as always. The local kids often passed through her yard as a shortcut, but rather than being annoyed, today she was thankful, because she didn't have to set the bag down.

The smell of pine suddenly floated toward her like a sad sweet dream and she wondered if the shepherd had ever smelled anything so clean, so pure.

Walking to the far end of her backyard, she stopped before the holly she had planted. She couldn't help but think how strange it was that human beings could bring life into this world in so many ways and yet had so little control over it in others.

She dropped to her knees and rolled the bag from her arms, accidentally crushing some of the holly berries that had rolled onto the light layer of snow leaving a bloodred stain.

She tugged the bag away from the holly and sighed. "Now what?" she murmured.

She closed her eyes for a moment. She had survived so much in her lifetime. She told herself this was just another painful occurrence to endure, but for whatever reason, it seemed more climactic.

She took in a deep breath, rose to her feet and went over to the shed where Bob kept the gardening tools. She needed a shovel.

Finding some still soft earth, Rose pushed on the shovel until it went into the ground. As she continued digging the hole, questions swirled through her mind. *Does everyone suffer, then die? Dogs and humans alike? Or is suffering meant to be stopped?*

"Mom?"

Her daughter's voice jolted Rose into reality. She spun around and stared at Emily, who stood in the middle of the backyard, her backpack slung on her left shoulder.

Emily, petite and blond, was wearing under her navy peacoat a gray skirt the same shade as the body bag that lay at Rose's feet. Rose winced and looked up, seeing the sky above her. Even the sky that seemed to hang so low, so heavy, was the same pale gray.

Rose dropped the shovel and began weeping.

"Mom. Oh my God, are you all right?" Emily ran toward her. "Mom, what's wrong? What is it?"

Rose felt Emily's arms wrap around her. She pressed her daughter closer, her grief spilling over.

"Mom, what's wrong?"

"I'm so glad you're here," Rose whispered. "I needed someone to hug the life back into me."

"You know I'll always be here for you. All you have to do is call." Emily lovingly rubbed her back, trying to soothe her. "I'm glad I stopped by to check on you."

Rose pulled away. "Why did you—"

"Bob called me and left a message on my machine asking me to check up on you. He sounded worried." Emily paused and looked toward the ground. "What's that?"

Rose looked over at the body bag. "It's a dog," she said quietly.

"A dog?"

Rose nodded.

"You mean a dead dog?"

"Yes. A dead dog."

Emily gawked at the bag, then at the open mound. "Mom, you're not going to bury it in our backyard, are you? I mean—"

"Emily, I have to. He has nowhere else to go." Rose picked up the shovel and leaning on it, turned to observe the hole she had dug.

"So . . . uh . . . who does it belong to?"

"No one. That's why he died."

"Oh, that's so sad." Emily approached the bag. "It was a he, huh?"

"Yes."

"Did he have a name?"

Rose shook her head.

"Well, let's give him one then. How about Hardwin?"

"Hardwin?"

"It means Brave Friend."

Rose felt a soothing warmth spread over her. The shepherd would have a name. And it suited him, too. "Hardwin. That's a good name."

"Mom, let me help you bury him."

Rose nodded, thankful to have been blessed with such a kind and caring daughter. Together, they lifted the gray bag and set it deep into the earthy bottom of the hole.

Dropping to her knees, Rose began pushing the dirt over the bag.

"Great-grandma would have said a few words about him," Emily murmured as the last of the dirt was patted into place.

"I know," Rose said. She twisted off some branches from the holly and a nearby white pine and set them on top of the grave, staring at the fresh mound they had made. Rose then looked over at Emily, who was brushing the dirt and snow from her winter coat and sighed.

Emily was only eighteen years old and yet, even with so few years, she knew so much. Perhaps because she had experienced so much. The divorce, moving from a comfortable home into a cramped one-bedroom apartment and Rose's grandmother's death so soon afterward. It was all so hard. For her and both her girls. "I'm glad you remember your great-grandmother."

Emily smiled, her cheeks dimpling. "Of course I do. Do you remember that one story she used to tell us about the time when an officer was going to shoot a lame horse, because it was blocking the street? She stepped right in front of that horse and told the officer that he was going to have to shoot her first. Great-grandma was a lot like you."

Rose smiled at the memory of her grandmother's story. "She was only ten when she stepped in front of that horse. What an amazing woman she was. All ninety-two years of her. I sure do miss her."

"Yeah. Me, too." Emily brushed a wisp of her blond hair from her cheek.

They were quiet for a moment.

"Let's say a prayer like great-grandma would."

"A prayer?"

"For the dog. We have to say a prayer. She'd say it isn't a proper funeral without one."

Rose looked toward the fresh mound of dirt and seeing the holly and pine boughs that surrounded it felt her heart lurch. No, it wouldn't be a proper funeral without a prayer. "I guess I just don't know what to say."

"I'll say it then." Emily folded her hands. "Dear Lord, take Hardwin into your arms and forever keep him there. For in your arms he will find the peace he was always looking for. While in your arms, as in our hearts, he will live forever more. Amen."

Rose closed her eyes and echoed, "Amen."

Emily turned toward her. "So. Where did you find him?"

Rose sighed. "Let's go inside."

Emily nodded.

"I'll make some tea and we'll talk," Rose added.

Emily took her mother's hand and they silently walked toward the house leaving behind the smell of pine.

❧ ❧ Chapter 9

Looking for Shelter

That Saturday, when the receptionist from the clinic called Rose to say the puppy was ready to go, Bob was still on the road. Rose drove quickly, purposefully to the veterinary clinic.

"I missed you, sweetie." Rose rubbed the small black head that nuzzled her arm as she carried the puppy out of the clinic. "I'm sorry I wasn't able to save your buddy. He was a good pal, wasn't he?"

The dog let out a low whimper as if he understood and Rose felt another twinge of sadness. Although she tried as best she could to push away thoughts of Hardwin, she couldn't. In fact, she had slept very little the past two days. Not even a phone call from her daughter cheered her up.

"I should give you a name, shouldn't I?" she murmured, pausing before her van.

She opened up the back door and paused to look down at the puppy in her arms. He had to know his buddy was gone. He whimpered again and squirmed.

His hind paws pushed at her as he tried to break free.

She laughed. "You squirm a lot, don't you? How about we call you Wiggles?"

He barked, still trying to wiggle loose.

"Wiggles it is. Come on. We're going to find you a home." She placed the dog on the backseat and closed the door. Getting into the driver's seat, she sighed, still feeling guilty about the decision she had reached to put Wiggles into a shelter.

She wanted to keep him desperately, but with her work it was impossible and with two girls in college she had no choice but to work. Her two cats were all she could handle right now. Except for a few scratches on the furniture, Peaches and Scooter were pretty low maintenance. And that's what she needed right now. Low maintenance. Just a few days away from the office had put her weeks behind in her accounting work.

"I'd keep you, Wiggles," she wistfully said. "You know I would, but with my job I wouldn't be able to give you much attention. And you need lots of attention after everything you've been through. Besides, Peaches, that's one of my cats, she hates dogs. There is no way you'd be able to even stay in the same room with her. She scratched the neighbor's dog so badly a few months ago he had to get stitches."

Rose had hardly pulled out of the parking lot when Wiggles squeezed between the front seats. A laugh escaped Rose when she looked over and found him comfortably seated beside her, his stubby tail hitting the base of the seat.

"My two girls used to fight over the front seat. Lucky for you they're all grown up or you would never have stood a chance." She sighed. "I haven't had Emily or Margaret in the front seat in a while. They're in college. But I have you, right? Or at least for a little while. I'm going to have to take you to a shelter." She looked over at him sadly. "They'll find you a nice home. I'll make sure of it."

And so it was that during the whole forty minutes it took to get to the RockaPet Shelter, Rose talked to Wiggles. It reminded her of the days she used to talk to her daughters when they were small. She liked to think of it as nonsense talk. It didn't matter what sort of talk it was, intelligent or not, it made her feel like someone who cared was listening. And that's all that mattered.

"We're here," she announced as she parked the car. "The best shelter in town. Or so my veterinarian told me. Okay. Out we go."

Inside, a short, plump woman with wiry red hair handed Rose a clipboard and a form filled with questions. With the clipboard in one hand and Wiggles in the other, Rose felt like she was juggling.

She plopped Wiggles on his feet while she sat down with the clipboard and tried to answer the questions as quickly as she could. *How old is the dog, approximately? Has the dog had shots? If so, what kind? What is the dog's medical history? Why are you bringing the dog in? Has the dog been spayed or neutered? Has the dog been treated for heartworm? Any other life-threatening diseases? Do you know the breed or mix of breeds of the dog? Has the dog any history of abuse?*

Rose chewed the end of the pencil, trying to come up with an answer for every question. She knew more about Hardwin's life than she did about Wiggles'. Wiggles could have been part of a litter belonging to a stray. He could have been dropped off in the neighborhood, left to die. Who knew what his history was?

"Your dog's eating the dirt from that pot over there," the woman at the desk drawled.

Rose jumped up and snatched Wiggles, who was gnawing at the soil of a potted ficus plant. "Yuck. You don't want that." She cradled him in her arms and brushed off the dirt that had gathered around his mouth. He licked his lips and wagged his tail. Rose bit her lip. Perhaps little Wiggles had been reduced to eating dirt for days at a time. Perhaps that was part of his history.

"Do you want me to put him in a cage for you until you're finished?" the receptionist asked.

"No, that's all right. He's not bothering me."

"If you say so. Just keep him away from the plant."

Rose set Wiggles down again, picked up the clipboard

and completed the last few questions. Handing it over to the receptionist, she patiently waited for the woman to go through her answers.

"He's at the pot again," the woman pointed out, glancing up at Rose.

Rose laughed and ran over to Wiggles. "You silly dog. Don't do that. You'll get sick."

She wiped his mouth again, remembering a time long ago when her daughter Margaret kept putting dirt into her mouth. Children weren't that different from puppies, were they? Both needed caring parent figures to guide them until they matured. She smiled and decided to keep Wiggles in her arms.

"So when do you think you'll find him a home?" Rose asked the red-haired woman as she walked up to the desk.

The woman looked up from the work she was doing and folded her hands as if she were about to deliver a speech. "The way things are going here, we might not even be able to take him in."

"You mean, I might have to take him somewhere else? I called yesterday and you said I could bring him in."

"He's a puppy. That's the only reason we'd accept him. Puppies are almost always adopted. Older dogs or dogs with health problems often have to be put down, because no one wants to adopt them and we don't have the space or resources to keep them indefinitely. If you wanted to bring in an older dog, I would have told you not to come. Now please be patient. We're currently understaffed."

" 'Currently understaffed,' " Rose repeated. That was the same thing one of the other shelters told her when she had called looking for help for the German shepherd. "Now, when you say understaffed, what does that mean?" she ventured. "And how long does *currently* last?"

The woman sighed and gathered some of the scattered papers on her desk. "A shelter runs just like a business. Except, in this business, there aren't any financial gains. Only dog gains. People like you come in all the time. We have no control over the number of dogs that come in or when we're filled to capacity."

The phone beside the woman rang. "Excuse me for a moment." She picked it up. "Hello, RockaPet Shelter. This is Rita."

Wiggles started pushing at Rose's arms, insisting on being released. She gently rubbed the side of his neck, hoping to calm him.

"I'm sorry, sir," the woman said into the phone, scratching her head with a long red fingernail. "We can't help you. We're currently understaffed." With that she hung up.

Rose eyed Rita and wondered whether she did that every time someone who had an adult dog called looking for help. "What was the call about?" she asked, leaning toward the woman.

"A stray, as always."

"And you couldn't help?"

Rita rolled her eyes and stood up. "Look. We only have one investigator and he's out sick. The investigator is usually the one that goes and looks into those things."

"You should really have another investigator," Rose pressed. "You shouldn't wait. Do you know the kind of shape these dogs are in? They really need help."

"There are other shelters people can call."

Disgusted, Rose leaned over the counter and snatched up one of the papers Rita had been working on for Wiggles. "I'll be better off searching for a home for Wiggles myself. For all I know, he'll end up dying in here waiting for you to get your act together. You know, your attitude doesn't help in finding these dogs the right homes."

"Do you want to file a complaint?" the woman challenged.

"A complaint? No." Rose shook her head. "I don't think that'll help. They're probably filed in the wastebasket. Just remember this: Every time you say no to someone who's looking for help, a dog may end up dying."

And with that, Rose walked out, propping Wiggles against her shoulder.

"Don't worry, Wiggles," she assured him, patting his back. "I know you need the right kind of home. A really nice home. Big couches for you to lie on, big bones for you to chew, cotton slippers for you to rip apart and all the good things in life a dog deserves." She blinked back tears. She'd never realized how mistreated stray dogs were. Even shelters either turned them away or gassed them to death. Those poor creatures needed someone to speak for them, someone to protect them, to take care of them and their needs. And she wanted to be that someone, the one Hardwin had needed when he was chained to that oil drum. But where was she to start? How could she help?

When she got to her car, she put Wiggles in the front seat beside her, knowing he'd be content there. "There's only one place to take you," she said, feeling happy but anxious. "Let's go home."

"Don't make me lock you in the bathroom!" Rose warned Peaches, who hadn't stopped hissing at Wiggles since she had brought him home. "Why are you so mean, anyway? He hasn't even so much as barked at you."

Peaches hissed again, swatted a paw in Wiggles' direction, then sprinted into the kitchen.

"You're acting like a brat," Rose called after her.

Wiggles gazed curiously after Peaches, got up and followed her into the kitchen.

"Don't do it, Wiggles," Rose called, standing up. "She's evil when it comes to dogs!"

But Wiggles continued on his way, wagging his tail behind him. Rose shook her head. When was he going to learn?

From the kitchen came hissing, barking, shuffling, more barking, then the sound of a huge crash. A toy flew out of the kitchen and into the living room and then it was quiet. Complete silence. That made Rose even more nervous than the ruckus. She ran into the kitchen and stopped short.

There were Peaches and Wiggles sitting together in Wiggle's new dog bed. Of course, Peaches was still hissing, but Wiggles obviously didn't take her too seriously. "Well, that's a start," Rose laughed.

❧ ❧ Chapter 10

A Small Deposit

"Rose! Rose, what the hell is this?"

Rose walked into the living room and saw Bob standing in the entryway staring down at little Wiggles with an expression she could only describe as complete horror.

"Hello to you, too," she said, coming toward him. "How was your trip?"

"Don't change the subject. I've only been gone three days and I come home to find a dog here! What's going on?"

She didn't reply.

"You know," he said, looking more closely at the furry ball that was sniffing his shoes, "he looks like that puppy we took out of that neighborhood. Is this...is this the same dog?"

"Bob, he had nowhere else to go," she firmly stated.

"I don't want another animal in this house, especially a dog." He leaned down, pushing the puppy away from his feet and sighed heavily. "I thought I made my feelings clear."

"Bob, please."

He shook his head and walked past her. "I'm going to get something to eat. Come with me. I want to talk to you."

Rose bent down and took up the puppy, rubbing his little head. "It's nothing personal, Wiggles. He's always grumpy when he gets home from one of his trips."

"I heard that," Bob called from the kitchen. "You wanna keep him? Go ahead and keep him. But I'm not taking care of that dog, you understand?"

"I understand." She went over to the cage she had set up for Wiggles until he was trained, gently put him in and then walked slowly to the kitchen. "The only hard part about taking care of a dog is housebreaking it. And he's been doing pretty good." She looked at Bob who had opened the refrigerator.

"Where's all the food?" he asked, bending over and peering into the refrigerator. "There's not a damn thing in here."

"I've been really busy," she said.

"You what? Well, do you think you could find an hour in the day to fill our fridge with food?" he snapped. "What am I supposed to eat?"

"I'll go shopping," she said as they walked back to the living room. "I have a few errands to run anyway."

"So I'm already taking care of him," he said, pointing at the puppy that was now barking from inside the cage.

"All you have to do is put him outside when he whimpers. It means he needs to do his business. I'll be back to feed him and play with him. Is that all right?"

"Yeah, fine, fine. Go."

Rose paused at the front door and looked back at Bob. He walked over to the cage, peered inside and reached his fingers through the bars to pat the dog's little head. Rose left with a smile on her face. She was sure things would be just fine.

That night they went to bed in silence. Of course, neither could sleep. Finally, Rose nudged him. "Bob."

There was a deep silence on the other side of the bed, then a cough. "Yeah?" he finally asked.

"I . . . I have a problem."

He laughed. "Right. So why are you telling me? I'm not a shrink. I'm just a truck driver with uppity ideas of owning a fleet, remember?"

Rose took a deep breath. "Look, Bob, I'm sorry about what happened at the clinic when I found out Hardwin died."

"Hardwin?"

"The German shepherd. Emily named him. Anyway, I didn't mean to blame you or yell at you or...I just...I lost it. I'm sorry. I've never experienced anything so...well, so overwhelmingly unfair. And when I couldn't find a shelter for the puppy, I didn't know what to do."

"Right."

They were both quiet and Rose felt increasingly uncomfortable. She hated depending on anyone, especially someone who wasn't an animal lover like she was. Of course, she didn't know anyone who loved animals as much as she did.

"You still there?" he asked.

"Yeah." She hesitated. "The truth is no one wanted to take Wiggles and I just gave up and brought him home. What else was I supposed to do?"

"Wiggles?"

"The puppy. I named him Wiggles."

"Well, it suits him," he said grudgingly.

"He likes it," she replied defensively. "And so do I."

Rose cleared her throat and forced herself to get to the point. "You know, all my life I've felt I was put here for a reason and maybe these abused animals are supposed to be a sign. Bob, I want to save suffering dogs."

"You want to save dogs." He sighed. "Listen, Rose, if you really want to help these animals, I suggest you volunteer at some of the shelters. It's obvious they need all the help they can get."

"I'm aware of that, but I don't think that will take me in the direction I want to go. I want to be out there, like we were that night and really save dogs."

"Rose, I don't think it's a good idea to get this involved. If you're not careful, you'll only end up—"

"What do you mean, you don't think it's a good idea?" She nervously chewed the inside of her cheek.

"The way you reacted at the clinic tells me you're not emotionally prepared to deal with the kinds of problems these animals have. It's noble to want to go out and rescue dogs, but it's obvious that when it comes to dogs, you can't control your emotions."

Rose ran a shaky hand down her nightgown, smoothing the wrinkles. "I know I can get emotional, but I feel I have to get involved, Bob. After what happened to Hardwin, I just don't think I could live my life knowing that I didn't try to help animals that need me." She shook her head. "I just want to save neglected and mistreated animals. Don't make me out to be crazy. I'm not."

"No, I wouldn't say you're crazy. Hell, I think I'm the one that's crazy or I wouldn't have helped you with those dogs."

Hearing the exasperation in his voice that he tried to mask with humor, Rose asked, "Hey, how about I take you out to dinner tomorrow night so we can talk more about this?"

"Oh, so you're asking me out on a date?"

She half smiled. It sure sounded like that, didn't it? Geez. They hadn't gone anywhere in ages.

"Yes, Bob. I'm asking you out."

He shook his head. "I'll say yes to dinner but don't think you're going to talk me into anything else."

She withheld a smile. He had a big heart beneath that trucker facade. "Chito's at seven then?"

That night they snuggled like spoons.

The next morning, however, when Wiggles, who had somehow gotten out of his cage, left a small deposit next to the bed, they began arguing again.

"Look, Rose, as much as I love you I don't want you getting involved in this stray dog business any more than you already are."

They argued all morning until she had to leave for work. And when she got home that evening, Bob had already left. She hoped that despite their angry words that morning, he was still going to meet her for dinner.

At the restaurant, Rose was surprised to find a clean-shaven husband in a nice, crisp polo shirt and khakis. She never even remembered him owning such nice clothing. And she did his laundry. He looked good.

Bob strode toward her. "I was hoping you'd arrive soon."

He led her to a booth. They sat down and stared at each other across the table as if they had never seen one another before.

Bob picked up his fork and absentmindedly began fiddling with it. "So, uh, how are you doing?" he finally asked.

"Better. Not a whole lot better, but better." She watched him continue to play with his fork.

"Good." He put his fork back onto his napkin and started poking at his spoon. "I'm still getting used to the idea of you wanting to help dogs. What are we talking here?"

Rose leaned across the table, wanting him to look at her. "What if I asked you to help me? Would that change how you feel?"

He shifted in his seat, scooting further into the booth. He seemed agitated. "Help you with what exactly?"

Rose wondered if she was making him nervous. It had been a while since they had sat down and had any sort of real conversation. She leaned back to give him his distance. "Helping dogs."

Bob picked up the glass of water in front of him and started drinking. Half the water was gone before he set it down. He pushed the glass aside and shifted in his seat again, looking around. "Where's the waitress?"

"Bob, I asked you a question," she said, leaning farther back into her seat. "I take it this whole thing about the dogs makes you nervous?"

He drummed his fingers against the table and shifted in his seat again. "No. What makes you think that?" He picked up a spoon and started twirling it in his fingers.

She leaned over the table and took hold of his fidgeting fingers. "You haven't been able to sit still since we sat down."

He pulled his hand away and set aside the spoon he was holding. "I'm just worried about where all this'll lead."

"Where do you think this is going to lead?"

He picked up his napkin and started unfolding it. "Divorce."

"Divorce?" She felt as if she had been hit in the stomach. "Why would my helping abused animals lead to our divorce?"

"Because it's obvious you're unhappy about your life," he drawled, leaning out of the booth and looking around. "Where's the waitress?"

"I'm sure she'll be here in a moment."

"I hate waiting." He picked up his glass of water and finished it off.

"Bob," she softly said, leaning into the table again, "I'm trying to reach out to animals that need help. Is that wrong?"

"Of course not." He pushed aside the silverware to the far end of the table. "It's just how you go about it."

Rose fingered the base of the glass before her. She was hoping this "date" of theirs would go well. But by the looks of things, she'd be lucky if he even talked in sentences.

"If there's anyone who I wish would understand," she slowly said, "why I want to do this, it's you. I mean, if you saw a child hurt on the street, would you walk by?"

"Listen, Rose." He shifted in his seat again. "You're confusing your responsibility with the responsibilities of others. I mean, you talk about if I would walk by a hurt kid. Hell no, you know I wouldn't. But that doesn't mean I'm going to be out on the street looking for hurt kids and taking them home. Do you understand what I'm saying?"

Rose looked at him, silently imploring him to understand, but his blue eyes were focused on the crushed napkin in his large hand. "Bob, couldn't you bring yourself to understand?"

He placed the white napkin onto the table and began ironing it out with both hands. "I don't know. I just don't know." He scooped up the napkin again and crushed it in his fist.

"I love you, Bob. You know that, don't you?"

He released the napkin he was torturing in his hand and nodded.

"It would mean a lot to me if you'd help me from time to time with this. It's obvious there aren't a lot of people wanting to help these dogs."

"Hey, if you want to go to battle, that's fine. But you're not dragging me into it." He leaned over the table and pointed at her water. "You going to drink that?"

She pushed it toward him. "No, take it."

"Thanks." He picked it up and swallowed the contents of the glass within a few seconds. He set the glass down and looked around again. "When that waitress shows up, order a tostada for me, will you? No spicy sauce. I have to use the men's room."

He got up and disappeared toward the back of the restaurant. Rose looked at the two empty glasses on the table and sighed. Of course he had to go to the bathroom.

"Can I take your order?" the waitress asked, coming up to the table. "Or would you like me to wait until he gets back?"

"Uh, no, I'll order," Rose quickly said, picking up the menu. "He'll have a tostada, hold the hot sauce."

"And you?"

"I'll uh . . ." She looked over the menu. "I'll have the same. Oh, and two more waters." She pointed to their empty glasses.

The woman nodded and went to get a pitcher of water. Just as she was filling their glasses, Bob returned.

"I'll have a tostada, no hot sauce," he said, sitting down.

Rose tucked two hands beneath her chin. "I already ordered."

"Oh." He nodded to the waitress and went back to playing with his silverware.

"Maybe I can talk you into seeing the neighborhood where I want to help the dogs live again?"

He picked up his glass of water and started drinking again, avoiding her gaze.

"Bob, come on. It's not like I'm asking much. I'd only ask for help when I couldn't handle things on my own."

"I don't want you going into that neighborhood ever again," he insisted. "If you're going to save dogs, save them in our neighborhood."

"Bob—"

"I don't want to hear about it anymore."

"Bob, please."

"No."

Rose sighed. So much for him understanding. But she wasn't going to give up on her idea. She didn't need him to rescue dogs. Maybe it was best she just keep Bob out of it. He was on the road almost all the time anyway.

Their meal came and they ate in silence. Occasionally, she looked up at Bob, hoping to make eye contact, but every time she did, he looked away, his face hard and unmoving.

On the way to work the next morning, Rose stopped in Dalton City and took out some of the dog food she'd bought the day before, scattering it on the side of the road. She had done this for three other days and the food always disappeared, so she was sure some animals were eating it.

She grabbed the box of small, plastic bags she had brought and walked over to little Mike's house hoping she could get his help. She knocked on the door. No one answered. She sighed and went back to her van. Opening the back door, she began popping off the lids on the cans of dog food one after another. She then yanked out twenty sandwich bags. *That should be enough food for a few days*, she figured.

"Moist and Meaty, here we go." It was the only brand of

dog food she had found which had water as a main ingredi-
ent and she knew water was probably more important for
these poor animals than food itself.

She dropped the contents of the packet into the open bag,
set it aside and took up another bag. Every now and then,
she spilled chunks of dog food onto the ground. She
brushed them aside with her foot and kept right on filling
the bags. She didn't realize how much work went into filling twenty of them.

"Hi."

Rose looked up to see little Mike standing there watching her with large brown eyes.

"Hi, Mike." She scrambled to her feet, wiping her hand
on her pants. "You know, I knocked on your door just a few
minutes ago. No one answered."

"Grandma was getting dressed and I was getting ready
for school." He shifted his knapsack on his shoulder and
looked at the bags on the sidewalk. "Are those for the
dogs?"

"Yes." She bent down and started gathering them. "You
want to help me drop them off?"

He shook his head. "I can't. Gotta go to school." He
paused and then eyed Rose suspiciously, saying,
"Grandma said people around here are fussing over some
lady in a van throwing food out the window."

Rose couldn't help but smile. "That lady would be me."

"Oh. Well, I know it's for the dogs, but people here don't
like it. You see that house?" He pointed at the red brick
house on the corner where Rose was going to make her
first drop of food. "The man who lives there grabs up all
the food you put by his house."

"You mean the dogs haven't been getting any?" she
asked in disbelief.

He sighed. "Not the stuff you put near that guy's house,
but there are packs and packs of dogs around here. Some of
them are getting something."

"Packs and packs of dogs?"

He nodded.

"That's it." With a few filled bags in her hands, Rose angrily headed toward the house that Mike had pointed out. There was no way she was going to let some jerk starve these animals.

As if she had called him forth, a pale-skinned man with an obviously fake hairpiece perched on his head opened the front door of the red house and stepped out. Rose kept going, determinedly gritting her teeth and telling herself not to be frightened.

"Hey," the man yelled, coming down the stairs. "Are you the one always dropping them bags of dog food by my house?"

"Yes," she said, heading toward him.

"I already got animal problems," he said, drawing closer. "I got dogs, cats, raccoons, mice, rats. You name it and I got it. I don't want to see you dropping off food for them on my block ever again. You got that? Let them critters die for all I care. There's too many of them as it is."

Rose waited until he was standing right in front of her before she said, "There's no law against feeding dogs."

"You want me to call the cops?" he yelled, pointing toward the house. "Is that what you want?"

"Go ahead. As I said, there's no law saying I can't feed starving dogs." She showed the man the plastic bags she was holding. "I'm going to put these bags on this corner and you're not going to touch them. You touch them and I'll bring more. Someone has to take responsibility for these poor dogs. From what I understand, there are packs and packs of them starving."

The man stared at her as if she were insane. "I'm calling the cops."

"Go right ahead." She walked past him and headed toward the corner. She placed four bags on the grass, a foot apart. She stood there several minutes to show she couldn't be bullied, then sauntered back toward her van.

As soon as the house was out of sight, Rose ran toward Mike who had gathered the remaining bags of food. "I have to go, Mike," she quickly said. "Let me have those." She pointed to the bags.

"He's calling the cops, isn't he?"

"Yeah, I think so. That's why I have to go." She grabbed the bags from Mike's arms and hurried toward her van with him following her.

"Could you open the door for me?" she asked, stopping next to the van.

Mike yanked the door open.

"Thanks." She dumped the bags of food onto the passenger seat and got in the car. "And hey, do me another favor." She hurriedly dug into her purse and pulled out one of her business cards. "If you see any dogs that need help, you call me."

He nodded and took the card from her.

"I'll treat you and your grandma to lunch sometime soon, okay? Bye!"

She pulled away from the curb, then rolled down the window. No toupee-covered jerk was going to scare her from feeding hungry dogs. She leaned over as best she could, the car still moving, and hastily gathered bags with her right hand. One after the other, she hurled them out the window.

❧ ❧ Chapter 11

Eerie Silence

No sooner had Bob gone back out on the road with a long-distance delivery the next Saturday, than Rose grabbed her purse and got into the van, determined to go back to Dalton City and talk to Elspeth and little Mike.

Since Bob was going to be gone for over a week, she figured she'd be able to use that time to feed her new charges, an activity of which he certainly wouldn't have approved. They had travelled beyond the point of miscommunication and had become silent adversaries. She had begun to realize that the heart of their conflict was the fact that they were so different. She tried not to think of their marriage and where their relationship was heading.

Rose first drove to the PetSmart. She wanted to be prepared the next time she found dogs like Hardwin and Wiggles. She didn't want to feel helpless again or feel as if she needed to depend on Bob or anyone else to save them.

She grabbed a shopping cart, went inside the store and headed straight toward the back. It was still early in the morning and there were hardly any other shoppers. She grabbed case after case of moist dog food, bag after bag of dry food, collar after collar in all sizes, blanket after blanket, water bowls and whatever else she could think of that would have been useful that first day with Hardwin.

She pushed the full cart to the front of the store and parked it next to the register.

The teenage boy behind it looked at her overflowing cart and smiled. "I can help you right here."

"No, I'm not done yet." She headed past the register and grabbed another cart. "I've got a lot more to get."

Going down aisle after aisle, she searched for items she could use.

"Vitamins. Malnourished dogs need vitamins," she said to herself, pausing and looking at white boxes, yellow boxes, blue boxes. "Barley Dog supplements it is." She gathered four boxes at a time and threw a total of eight into the cart.

"We're probably going to have to get rid of worms, too," she commented, looking for something easy to administer. "D-Worm chewable tablets it is. Good price, too.

"Treats. I need treats." She turned the half-filled shopping cart to her right and skidded to a stop when she found what she was looking for. "Let's see."

She leaned close and decided to choose what looked the most appetizing. "Chops dog treats and Beggin' Strips." She rounded up some of each and plopped them into her cart.

"Can I help you find anything?" a woman's voice asked.

Rose turned and saw a gray-haired woman dressed in a vest with the store logo on it.

"Uh, yes." She twirled her cart toward the woman. "I was hoping to buy a cage and a carrier."

The woman nodded. "This way. As far as carriers go, the Furrari Three-Fifty Pet Carrier is the best way to go. Cages are more or less the same, just size differences."

Rose followed the woman toward the side of the store. She stopped when she saw a vast array of cages and carriers and grinned. "Thanks. I can take it from here."

The woman looked at her for a moment longer and then disappeared down the aisle.

"Furrari Three-Fifty Pet Carrier," Rose murmured, looking around. "Sounds like Ferrari to me." She located it, looked at the price tag and whistled. "One hundred and forty dollars. It's a Ferrari all right."

She sighed and pulled it from the shelf. It would pay for itself eventually. "In you go."

When the second cart was full, she turned it around and headed back to the front of the store to make room for more things. She parked the cart next to the other one piled with food.

The cage and then I'm done, she thought, heading back to the aisle where she had found the carrier. She examined the cages, trying to decide which was best and finally pulled the one which looked most comfortable off the shelf.

Two carts full and a carrying cage after she had gone through the store, she was almost ready to check out her purchases when she decided to ask about canned food. She didn't feel five cases were enough. "You wouldn't happen to know if you stock more of this food, do you? I'd like six more cases."

The freckle-faced teenager behind the register gave a laugh. "Why don't I get it for you." He came back a few minutes later lugging the cases and started ringing them up. "How many dogs do you have anyway?" he asked, passing the items over the scanner as fast as he could.

"They're not really my dogs," she nimbly replied. "I'm trying to help out stray dogs."

"Wow, that's great. If I had a lot of money, I'd be doing the same thing. I love dogs."

Rose grimaced as she watched the growing tally on the register screen. She really didn't have a lot of money, but she had just gotten a large bonus and she had credit cards—with limits, of course. She didn't even want to think about how much the bill would total.

The boy leaned over the counter, looked at the remaining items in Rose's carts and leaned back. "Man, I don't think I ever rang up this much stuff even in a week."

Rose continued piling the items on the counter, toppling some of them. "I think you need a bigger countertop."

He laughed and kept on scanning. "Not everyone shops like you do."

She smiled and nervously watched as one of the other employees came up and started helping bag the order. *They probably think I'm some kind of nut,* Rose thought, looking around at the immense quantity of merchandise and food she was purchasing.

She pushed collars and leashes toward the scanner and piled the boxes of vitamins and heartworm pills on top of each other. In the more or less empty store, the scanner seemed to beep louder than usual, drawing as much attention as a screaming person. Another employee came by, bringing with her two empty carts, and she also started bagging.

Finally, everything had been rung up. "And your grand total," her friend the cashier announced, "and I mean grand, is one thousand, seven hundred fifty-three dollars and twenty-two cents." He grinned. "Cash or credit?"

"Credit," Rose stammered, trying not to feel like she had just sold her soul to the credit card company. She fumbled in her wallet for her Visa card and handed it to him.

He slid her card through the register. "Now this is going to be fun," he said.

The receipt started printing.

"It'll probably take a while." He grinned again. "Let's just hope we don't run out of paper."

Rose sighed, leaned on the counter and watched the receipt fold over and over again, only to be gathered up neatly by the teenager. Five minutes later, she was handed a roll that seemed to her like a huge package of toilet paper.

It took over an hour to load everything into the van. Then, having worked up an appetite on her shopping spree, Rose stopped at a fast-food restaurant before heading to Dalton City.

•   •   •

All was quiet in southeast Dalton City, as it always seemed to be. From time to time, a car drove by and a car door could be heard opening and slamming closed. There were few pedestrians. A rusted part fell off an old green car that had been parked on the street since she'd begun to go there, but otherwise, silence prevailed.

And then she saw them. They were just as little Mike had described: a pack of dogs, both small and large, mostly mixed breeds and all searching eagerly for food.

As she sat down on the curb to fill plastic bags with dog food, Rose watched the pack meander toward one of the abandoned buildings. If they had noticed her, it was only out of the corners of their eyes. Whatever the reason, they weren't heading in her direction.

A bearded homeless man pushing an overflowing shopping cart interrupted her thoughts as he walked down the side of the road. He didn't seem to notice her, just stared straight ahead and pushed on. As she watched the man, she suddenly realized why these strays came to this particular area. The homes and people were as dilapidated and pitiful as they were.

She tossed the bags she was holding in the direction the dogs had gone and headed back toward the van. If only there was more she could do. It seemed almost senseless to continue feeding these animals when so many were in need of medical care and loving homes.

A loud yelp suddenly pierced the silence around her. She froze, her hand resting on the van door and then turned to see where it had come from. It sounded like a dog. A dog in pain.

"You good for nothing son of a—"

Another yelp interrupted the angry voice.

Rose moved away from the van and edged past a large tree that was blocking her view. She caught her breath just as a bald-headed man sent a boot to a light brown dog who resembled a golden retriever. It was so skinny it looked as if it was having trouble standing.

The man kicked the dog again. Whatever the dog had done, it didn't deserve to be kicked. Another yelp escaped the dog.

Rose's throat tightened as the man grabbed the dog by what appeared to be a steel collar and yanked him off the ground. The dog whined and cried, pleading to be set down. Its paws dangled in the air searching for stability.

The man threw the dog on the ground.

The dog trembled, keeping its head low, but did nothing else.

If the man weren't so big and frighteningly angry, Rose would have approached him and told him to stop. But she was just as scared as the dog was.

He grabbed the dog and dragged him toward the side of the house. They went around to the back and disappeared from view.

Rose was standing in the middle of the street now, knowing she couldn't walk away from what she had just witnessed.

"He always kicks that dog," someone behind her said.

She turned. It was the homeless man she had seen earlier. He was looking at her as if he knew what she was thinking. He sniffed, adjusting the black hat on his head and looked toward the house as if waiting for the man to come back out.

"He does that all the time?" she quietly asked.

"Yep. And if he keeps beating on that dog the way he does, it's not going to make it, that's for sure. Last time he took a shovel to its back. I thought for sure he broke it."

Rose placed a hand over her mouth.

"You're the one feeding all them dogs all the time?" the man asked, eying her.

She nodded.

"Oh, them dogs do love it. You see 'em waggin' them tails fast every time they find that food. That's real nice. Why d'you do it?"

"Because I don't want them to die."

"Then why don't you just pick 'em up? Ain't no sense in feedin' 'em once and lettin' 'em starve the rest of the time."

A yelp from the backyard interrupted their conversation and Rose's head jerked back toward the house.

"He's probably tryin' to chain him again. Real tight." The man put two grimy hands to his throat demonstrating. "He's gonna choke that dog to death one of these days. One link too many'll do it."

Rose couldn't help but think of Hardwin. Hardwin had been chained in the same manner, and she'd be damned if she let another dog suffer the same fate.

"You wouldn't happen to have any change, would you?" he suddenly asked, leaning toward her. He stank of alcohol.

Although Rose, remembering her alcoholic mother and first husband, didn't want to promote his addiction, she felt that he had done her a favor. "Hold on." She ran over to her car and pulled out a five-dollar bill from her wallet.

She ran back over to him and gave it to him. "Here."

He looked at the bill she had given him and shoved it into his pocket, a big smile coming over his bearded face. "Thanks. This is more than I need." He patted his pocket and went back to the shopping cart that he had left in the street.

Rose watched the homeless man rearrange some of the plastic bags in his cart and wondered what else he knew about the neighborhood.

"Hey," she called after him.

He turned.

"I'll give you ten dollars for every dog you tell me about."

He rushed toward her, his baggy pants shuffling. "Which dog do you want to know about? I see a lot of them walking around this neighborhood."

"Any one of them. Here, let me give you my number. Hold on." She ran back to her car and ripped off a sheet of paper from the pad attached to the mirror. Taking the pencil clipped to it, she wrote her number on the paper. Hurrying back to the man, she gave it to him. "Call me any time you see a dog that needs my help. You'll get ten dollars for every dog."

"So, uh, what's your name?"

"Rose."

"Rose. Well, it's nice to meet you, Rose. The name's Royce. You know, like the car?"

She smiled. "Right. Thanks, Royce. Don't hesitate to call."

"For ten dollars a dog? Don't you worry." He held up a hand in salute and headed back to his shopping cart.

Now that she had two spies in the neighborhood, maybe she could make some headway. Of course, the first dog she had on her agenda was the one she had just seen being beaten by his owner.

She got into her van. She'd go home and scan the pamphlets she had picked up from all the local shelters. Maybe she could find help somewhere. There were laws about animal abuse. Laws that should be enforced. No person could just beat a dog, starve it and chain it.

Just a few blocks away, Rose noticed a police car. She thought for only a moment before she flashed her lights and honked her horn. She pulled over and waved.

The police car immediately turned around and pulled up behind where she was parked. The cop got out.

She rolled down her window as he came up.

"Is something wrong?" the policeman asked, looking at her.

"I know this is probably not something you do every day, but is there any way you can take a dog off someone's property?" she asked.

He thought about it for a moment, then looked back at his car. "What are we talking about here?"

"I just saw this man brutally beating a dog and I know that can't be legal. I don't think he even feeds it—it was all skin and bones."

He nodded. "Yeah, we do that sort of thing from time to time. I think I have a dog pole in the back of my squad car. Where's this at?"

"Around Badger and Fuller."

The man whistled and shook his head. "Sorry. Out of my jurisdiction."

"You mean there's nothing you can do?"

"I can call another officer who covers that area to try to look into it."

"Could you?"

He nodded. "I'll do it now. I hope it works out. I hate to see animals suffering. Especially dogs."

"Thank you. I'll be there waiting."

Rose drove back to the neighborhood and parked. An hour passed, but no police car showed up.

"Damn it." She pulled out her cell phone and dialed 911.

"Nine-one-one," a man's voice responded. "What's your emergency?"

"Hi. I'm calling to report a man who was just beating his dog. Is there anything you can do?"

"And where are you located?"

"Badger and Fuller," she replied, double checking the street signs.

"And your number?"

"I'm on my cell phone."

"Your number?" the man repeated.

She sighed and gave it to him.

"I'll have someone call you right back."

"How soon?"

"Within fifteen minutes."

Rose slapped her phone shut and looked at her watch. It was already three in the afternoon. Where had the time gone?

A few minutes later, the phone rang.

"Hello?"

"Hi. This is Officer Brands calling in response to a dispatch."

Rose sat up and shifted in her seat. *Finally.* "Thank you for calling. I'm on Badger and Fuller and I want to report a man who was beating his dog. I'm worried he's going to kill him."

There was silence on the phone and then a stifled laugh.

"What's so funny?" she snapped, almost forgetting she was talking to a police officer.

"I thought this was a domestic abuse call."

"If it'll make you come down here, you can most certainly call it that," she icily replied. "This dog needs help and I can't just walk into the guy's backyard."

"So why don't you call animal control?"

"Animal control? But this dog needs help."

"Look. You calling me about this is like someone crying about a mouse she finds dead in a trap. I don't have time for calls like this. Maybe you should call the Humane Society." He laughed again. "Dog abuse. Now there's a real crime."

With that, the phone went dead. She shook her head in disbelief. Now what?

Rose looked toward the house her van had been sitting in front of for the past hour and a half. Someone was staring out at her through the window.

It was the bald man, the same man that had earlier beaten his dog. She looked away, pretending she didn't see him.

Maybe she should use her cell phone to call the Humane Society again. At least they might give her advice on what to do. She dialed information, got the number and placed the call.

"Humane Society. This is Ron."

"Hi, Ron. My name is Rose Block and I need to speak with someone who deals with animal abuse cases."

"I can take your information."

"You can? Great."

"What's your name again?"

"Rose."

"And your last name?"

"Block."

"What's your address and zip?"

Rose rolled her eyes. "Do I have to give you all this stuff?"

"You're filing a complaint. This is how it works."

"I see." She gave her address.

"And your phone number?"

She gave it.

"Okay. And who is it you're setting the complaint against?"

"It's more than just a complaint. I saw this guy kicking his dog and from what someone else told me, he's also beaten it across the back with a shovel."

"Do you know the man's name?"

She frowned. "No."

"His address then?"

"Yeah, I've got that." She leaned sideways and ignored the fact that the man was still watching her through the window. "Five-five-five-five East Fuller. He lives in southeast Dalton City. I don't know the zip."

"And what is this guy doing again that we should look into?"

"He's beating his dog. He's also starving it. It looked too weak and skinny to even stand. That dog isn't going to last very long."

"And what kind of dog would you say it is?"

"It looks a lot like a golden retriever, but I guess it's a mixed breed."

"Okay. Is there anything else we should know?"

She thought for a moment. "No. I don't think I know anything else about the dog or the man."

"That's fine. We'll send out one of our investigators to look into it. They'll take care of it."

Relief flooded her. "Great. How long do you think it'll take before they go to see the dog?"

"We have a lot on our books right now. I'd say next week."

"Next week! Are you kidding?" Rose shook her head. "Can't you send someone out this week?"

"I'm afraid not. We're definitely looking at next week. That's the soonest we have available as of now. Don't worry," the man assured her. "We'll get somebody down there. Is there anything else we can do for you?"

"No. No, thank you." She hung up the phone and leaned back in the seat, unhappy about the outcome of her call. Then again, she shouldn't have been surprised. She had gone through this before when she'd tried to get help for Hardwin when he was chained to the fifty-five-gallon oil drum.

Another week. And in the meantime, who knew what that vicious jerk would do to the dog?

Suddenly, Rose sat up, an idea hitting her. Maybe she could buy the dog from the guy. It was obvious he hated the dog. Maybe he'd sell it.

She grabbed her purse, got out of the van and walked up to the house.

The door opened the moment she knocked on it, as if he had seen her and was waiting.

"What do you want?" the bald man asked, towering in the doorway. She saw now he hadn't lost his hair because of Mother Nature; he shaved it.

She wasn't even going to try to lecture him about what he had done earlier. She simply got to the point. "I want to buy your dog."

"He's not for sale. Now get the hell out of here. I don't like you sitting in front of my house."

"Why don't you want to sell your dog?" she insisted. "It's obvious you don't want him."

"What I do with my dog is my business, you understand? Now, get the hell out of here." With that, he slammed the door in her face.

Fine. If that was the way he wanted to be about things, she would just go and take his dog. Nobody else was doing a damn thing about it.

She hurried toward her van and got in. She'd go home, have something to eat and come back at night, as she and Bob had done when they rescued Hardwin. She would get that dog no matter what.

It was past midnight when Rose returned to the brick house in southeast Dalton City. All the lights in the house were out. She quietly got out of the van, which she had parked around the corner, and headed toward the house, a dog pole in one hand and a beef sandwich she had picked up from one of the local restaurants in the other. She figured a beef sandwich would be a better way of luring a hungry dog than canned food. He'd be able to smell it right away.

As she crept along the side of the house, her breath coming in deep gasps, a light went on inside. She froze and pasted herself against the wall.

What if he caught her? She swallowed and didn't dare move. Maybe he was just getting a glass of water or something.

She heard the back door open and her heart almost exploded in her chest. Dashing toward the front of the house, she glued herself against the wall again.

He must have seen her. He must have been waiting for her. But she wasn't going to leave unless he came after her.

"You want the dog?" she suddenly heard a deep voice yell from the back.

She leaned over the side of the house and looked into the dark walkway. He was talking to her.

"Come get him!"

Not knowing whether she should trust him, she continued to stand frozen, staring down the walkway.

And then she heard it. The most horrible sound she'd ever heard in her life. A yelping, screaming and then a sort of gagging coming from the dog.

"Oh God," she whispered, tears springing into her eyes. *He's choking the dog. He's choking the dog to death.*

"Don't you want the dog?" he shouted over the dog's screams and chokes.

He knew there was nothing she could do. What could she do? She didn't have anything to protect herself or the dog, and for all she knew the man had a loaded gun and was waiting to point it at her head.

She stood sobbing, clutching the beef sandwich and dog pole against her chest.

Within moments, there were no more screams or choking or yelping. Just silence. Eerie, death-like silence.

She didn't know how or when she got into her van and drove away. She just knew that she would never be the same.

❖❖ Chapter 12

Sleepless Nights, Tortured Days

Rose stared at the dark outline of the ceiling above her. She hadn't been able to sleep since that night she heard the dog being choked to death. She hadn't even been able to go back into the neighborhood where it happened.

She squeezed her eyes shut and tried to focus on relaxing, but the haunting, chaotic sounds of the dog yelping, coughing and howling echoed within her frazzled thoughts. How could she do nothing, knowing there were dogs suffering and dying each and every day?

She sat up, threw the sheets from her sweat-drenched body and got out of bed. Bob was still away. She had thought sleeping in his pajamas would help comfort her, but it hadn't.

"Three in the morning," she murmured, walking past the lighted digital clock and going into the hallway near the kitchen.

She had to get her mind off what happened. But how? How was she going to survive in her everyday world after witnessing such cruelty?

Flicking on the kitchen light, she took a glass from the cupboard and went to the sink to fill it with water. The sight of dirty dishes piled high reminded her she was neglecting everything in her life. She sighed.

"I'm not thirsty," she muttered, setting the glass on the counter and retreating to the living room.

Large stacks of newspapers, newsletters and pamphlets pertaining to shelters, dog abuse and animal rights carpeted the living room floor, making it impossible for her to get to the couch without stepping on them.

She was trying to come to an understanding of what was legal and what wasn't and what she might be able to do and not do to change the abuse going on.

She plopped herself on the couch. Turning on the lamp next to her, she picked up a piece of paper on which she had earlier listed her concerns. Animal rights and ethics, animal cruelty, animal assistance, animal shelters, laws to safeguard animals and so on.

Despite all her research, she had so many questions and so few answers. Where did she start? How could she make a difference? She set down the list and picked up a pamphlet on a local shelter.

"Volunteer-based, we provide humane solutions to an overpopulated and neglected society of animals," she read aloud. She stared at the name of the organization. It was the same shelter to which she had gone to drop off Wiggles. The same shelter where the woman with red fingernails had told her many of the dogs were put down, because they didn't have the funds to keep them. "Humane solutions, meaning killing abused creatures," she commented in disgust, throwing the pamphlet aside.

She hadn't realized how hard it would be to find an organization that would be willing to help her get suffering dogs off the streets of Dalton City. But since most of them were non-profit and volunteer-based and working in their own communities, they didn't have the time, money or the extra people to help the dogs in the poor neighborhood with which she was dealing. A neighborhood where people left their dogs chained to oil drums and beat them because of rage and frustration about their own lives. Sadly, she knew southeast Dalton City was only one of many thousands of neighborhoods where animals were being abused across the world. How was she going to prevent all the cruel, uncaring people on this planet from killing and starving their dogs? The enormity of the problem exhausted her.

There was a shuffle and the patter of feet from the kitchen and the next thing she knew, Wiggles had pounced into her lap. She tossed aside the pamphlet and held Wiggles close, staring at the mound of papers with a sense of misery.

"I'm becoming obsessed," she whispered, pressing her nose into his fur. "I can't sleep, I can't eat, I can't even keep food in the house. And work . . . Oh God, work."

Rose looked over at her briefcase. She had brought it home to do some work Rick needed for Monday, but had been unable to concentrate. She shook her head. Rick was going to be furious. She hadn't done anything. She was too busy trying to read everything she could on abused dogs and tomorrow was Monday.

She sighed and mumbled, "I just have to get some sleep. Come on, Wiggles. You can sleep with me for the next few hours." She cradled him closer, turned off the light and shuffled back to the quiet darkness of her room. Lying down again, she willed sleep to come. But still it eluded her. Again she lay staring at the ceiling, her eyes burning and her body weak from lack of sleep. Wiggles, who had curled up at her feet, was already nodding off.

Rose turned on her side and closed her eyes. "No more dogs. No more dogs," she repeated like a mantra.

It was no good. She opened her eyes again and stared at the clock. She turned over and then flipped back. Each position she tried was just as uncomfortable as the last. "No more dogs," she repeated again.

Finally, exhaustion overcame her and her thoughts drifted. The next thing she knew, the phone was ringing, interrupting the fragile peace she had found.

Rose moaned and threw out a hand, trying to find the phone without looking.

"Hello?" she asked weakly, the side of her face buried in her pillow.

"Rose, it's ten o'clock. Where are you?"

She bolted up and saw light streaming into the room. "Rick!" she exclaimed. "Oh God, I'm so sorry. I'll be there in less than an hour."

"Did you finish putting together that account?"

"No. I'm sorry. I didn't get around to it. I've been really—"

"Rose, what's wrong with you? You haven't been yourself since that time you called in saying you'd hurt your leg. You forget this, you forget that and you come in late. It's so unlike you. You were the most conscientious person here. Is there something I should know? Your work is—well, it's substandard. Even when you're here you're not able to focus. If it was anyone else, I'd be giving them notice right now."

Rose closed her heavy eyes, wanting to go back to sleep. "Rick, I'm really sorry. You deserve better than what I've been giving you. I know that."

"I'm glad you agree. Now, when are you coming in?"

She rubbed her forehead and sighed. It was at that moment she realized that whatever it took to make a difference for those poor creatures, she would do. Her old life just wasn't working for her anymore and she would have to fashion a new one. "Rick, I just can't. I can't come in today and I can't come in in the future."

She drew in a shaky breath. She couldn't believe she was choosing to let her profession go. After all she'd sacrificed to move ahead, the long hours, the training. First as Rick's secretary, then after she'd completed night school, as his accountant.

But it no longer meant anything. Her job was getting in the way of committing herself to the mission she now saw should be her life's work. She couldn't ignore how she felt.

"Is this about wanting a raise? A vacation?" Rick asked.

"No, no," she said. How could she even begin to explain what she had been going through? "Rick, do you remember that day I called in to say I hurt my leg when I was supposed to be reviewing Mr. Halsey's account?"

"Yeah?"

"Well, I didn't. I lied."

"You lied? Why would you feel the need to lie to me?"

"Look. The truth is I found a dying dog and I didn't think you'd give me the day off to rescue a dog. So I lied to you. I did it for the dog."

"Okay. So what does this have to do with you quitting your job?"

"Do you remember that call I got about that dog dying?"

"Yeah."

"Well, ever since then, the only thing I've found meaningful is going out and helping other dogs in need. But just a few days ago when I was out feeding strays, I found something worse." She closed her eyes, willing herself not to cry over the dog that had been murdered. "I just can't let this go. I have to do what I can."

"So let me get this straight. You want to quit your job and become a veterinarian?"

She shook her head. "No, Rick. I want to help bring stray and abused dogs into shelters, find them homes and keep them from dying. Dogs are starving and being beaten to death as we speak."

"Are you serious?" he asked incredulous. "You're going to quit a job you've sacrificed so much for to save dogs?"

"Very serious."

"But how the heck are you going to make a living doing something like that?"

"I don't know. But I'll be doing something I feel matters. For the time being, I guess Bob will be the sole breadwinner. I only hope he'll accept that." She swallowed hard, thinking of what she could say to her husband and how he might react.

"Oh, hell, Rose, are you going through a midlife crisis? Damn it. Why now, when things are going so well? I mean, you can't just quit your job over some—some dogs! You just can't!"

"I can, Rick," she calmly replied. "I have to and I will. Not you or Bob or anyone else is going to stop me. I'll finish pulling together my paperwork. I'll have Mr. Valerie's account for the quarter and an outline of our position and drop it off for you as soon as I can."

"Rose, for heaven's sake," he pleaded. "What are you going to live on? You have two girls in college. Bob's just started his business. You need the money."

"I'll give up eating out. I'll give up buying new clothes for the next few years. I'll give up buying anything for the house that's not necessary, if I have to. It doesn't matter what I need to give up. What matters is that I save these dogs, because no one else is going to save them. You know, when my mother put me in an orphanage, everyone treated me as if I were a worthless stray. Maybe that's why this means so much to me. I don't want anyone or any animal labeled worthless like I was. Can you understand how I feel?"

Rick was silent.

She sighed. "Rick, you know I've always been dedicated to your company. But you have to understand. I have discovered my real dedication now lies elsewhere. I don't know what you'd call it, maybe a calling, a humanitarian effort, I'm not sure what. My grandmother once told me everyone is capable of doing something great in his or her lifetime to better the world. I believe this is my time to reach for that goal."

"Rose, I can't believe you're doing this. Maybe...hell, maybe you need a vacation. Is that it? I'll give you a month off, with pay. How about that? And when you get back, we can talk. Or at least give me two weeks' notice. You don't think one day is even—"

"Rick, I'm sorry, but I can't. I can't wait another day to get started. Not with what I've seen."

"And there's nothing I can do to change your mind?"

"Nothing."

He heavily sighed. "Man, I can't believe this. Who would have thought that you...ah, forget it. All I ask is that you get Mr. Valerie's account pulled together. I'll take care of the rest. God, what am I going to tell people? Quitting a solid, secure job to become a dog rescuer. No one's going to believe it."

Rose jumped out of bed, feeling suddenly rejuvenated, uplifted. "Then that's it. I'll have everything ready for you in a week or so. That I can promise. And, Rick, it's a wonderful job. You'll have a lot of people applying and if you want me to help interview or even train someone, just call."

"I'll see you tomorrow with all the account paperwork in order." He paused. "Whoever heard of a person quitting a job to go out and rescue dogs?" He laughed. "You're one heck of a crazy woman, Rose, you know that?"

She nodded. "Maybe so."

"Now don't be getting yourself into trouble with those dogs."

She took a deep breath and let it out. "I promise. And thanks, Rick. You're wonderful. Absolutely wonderful."

Late that afternoon, Rose returned to Dalton City for the first time since the awful night she had heard the man strangle his dog to death.

She began her usual task preparing the food. Finally, she had just about finished. She popped off the last lid of dog food and tucked it against the wall of a graffiti-covered building. Gathering the plastic garbage bag she had been throwing all the aluminum lids into, she tied the ends together and slung it over her shoulder. All the dogs in the neighborhood would have enough food for quite a while.

As she strode back to her car absentmindedly watching fresh snowflakes begin to fall, a loud yelp caught her attention. She froze and turned to see where it had come from. It sounded like a dog. Another dog in pain.

"You disgusting bastard. You're nothing but a useless male."

Another yelp interrupted the angry tirade. To Rose's

horror, she saw a woman hitting a small, skinny brown dog in the front yard of one of the brick houses on the block.

"You're supposed to signal you want to go out when you have to go to the bathroom!" the woman continued shouting. Her face was beet red and full of anger. "If you do your business inside the house again, I'll skin you alive, you understand?"

Rose's throat tightened as the woman grabbed the dog by the neck and shook it.

"Go! NOW!" she commanded in a voice that clearly terrified the animal.

The dog cowered, keeping its head low, but did nothing else. Rose remembered what the man had done to his dog when she tried to intervene and remained silent.

"You're gonna spend the night in the yard, you mutt!" The woman grabbed the dog and dragged him toward the back of the house.

"I never knew there were so many hideous people in this world," Rose muttered, moving toward the house. It was starting to snow. What was she going to do? It's not like a shelter would step in on this one. This dog had an owner. A very nasty owner, but nonetheless she was the owner.

"She always hits and shakes that dog," said a young voice behind her.

Rose's head jerked back and she saw Mike approach her. He was looking at her as if he knew exactly what she was thinking. He sniffed and looked toward the house, as if waiting for the woman to come back out.

"She does it all the time?" Rose asked, even more disheartened.

"Sure does. Grandma says the dog's probably gonna die the way she keeps hurting it."

Rose placed a hand over her mouth.

"I didn't see you for a while," he said. "You're back feeding all of them strays, aren't you?"

She nodded and looked down at him. Mike was a good ally to have. "That woman. She lives here?" she quietly asked.

"Yep. She's gonna chain the dog outside again, even with the snow coming." He shivered.

Rose couldn't help but think again of Hardwin being chained to the dented oil drum. There was no way in hell she was going to let another dog suffer such pain. Not if she could help it. "Thanks. You helped me out a lot, Mike. Tell your grandmother thanks again." She smiled and patted his unkempt hair. "You're a really good kid, you know that? And don't worry about the dog. I'm going to find him a new home."

Bright brown eyes looked up at her in wonder. "Really? How?"

"I can't tell you, buddy." She leaned toward him. "I don't want to get you involved. But let me just ask you one more thing. Do you know the dog's name?"

"Mutt."

"Mutt?"

"Yeah. Mutt."

"That figures."

"Are you gonna call the cops on her? Grandma says the cops won't do anything about it since the dog's that lady's property."

"No, I won't call the cops," she replied. "I know they won't help. I've tried. Instead, I'm going to do something which will...never mind. You run along. It's getting dark."

"I don't mind the dark."

"Well, I do. You don't want your grandma getting worried."

He shrugged and went on his way. Rose watched him and knew he'd be helping her again. He might be only ten, but he saw a lot of what went on in the neighborhood and, unlike others, he cared. Suddenly, she remembered the arrangement she had made with Royce.

"Hey, Mike!" she called after him.

He turned and stared at her with large eyes.

"Hey, how about I give you ten dollars for every dog you tell me about?"

His eyes widened and he ran toward her. "You don't have to do that, you know."

She dug into her back pocket and pulled out a ten-dollar bill. "Here. That's for telling me about Mutt."

He took the money. "Thanks. I wouldn't take it, but it'll really help Grandma."

Rose nodded, wishing she could give him more.

He darted away and disappeared into his house.

"He's a good spy," she murmured and began charting her plan to rescue the dog. She knew she'd need to come back after dark and bring a saw and some blankets. She had watched Bob set Hardwin free and was sure she could do it.

Precisely at eight that night, Rose drove back into Dalton City. When she got to the end of the block where she had witnessed the woman hitting her dog in the falling snow, she switched the car's headlights off. The snow had turned to slush making her drive more cautiously. She had gone over in her mind what she had to do a hundred times. There was no other way to save Mutt. Not after what she witnessed that awful night the other dog was killed by its owner.

As nervous as she was, her actions parking the car were steady and her thoughts were collected as she zipped up her black jacket, grabbed the bolt cutter and got out. There were shouting voices in the far distance and the barking of dogs. Everything appeared so different at night. Much of the decay and poverty were obliterated by the darkness. Lights glowed from some of the houses, signs of life more apparent than during the daytime.

As Rose neared her destination, she paused and looked around. She could still hear a voice yelling from a distance, although she couldn't make out what was being said.

"Here goes," she whispered to herself and headed around the house. She crept alongside it, trying not to make a sound, until she reached the backyard.

Luck was with her. The gate was open. She entered without hesitation and kept her fingers crossed that the dog wouldn't bark and alert the owner.

The brown dog lay in the slushy snow in the corner of the yard, tightly leashed to the fence. She had no doubt that the dog knew she was there, yet he didn't even bother to raise his head to look at her. Even when Rose approached, his head continued to lay tucked between his legs. His eyes, on the other hand, watched her carefully.

"Hello, Mutt," she whispered, drawing closer. "I'm going to find you a better place. I'm going to get you out of here. So, whatever you do, don't bite and don't bark."

Rose shakily placed the teeth of the bolt cutter on the chain and began cutting the links, the sound of metal echoing around her. She stopped every now and then to make sure she wasn't making too much noise and then continued cutting. After about ten minutes and a very sore arm, the chain came loose.

"I'll buy one of those power saws," she joked to the dog in a whisper. "That way, this will go more quickly."

Rose put her hand in her pocket and took out a dog biscuit she had brought. "Here you go." She held it out to him.

The dog sniffed the air, moved toward her and eagerly took the biscuit from her hand. "That's a good dog. Now, let's see if you'll let me pick you up."

She put her arms around him, expecting to get snapped at, but the dog was busy chewing on his biscuit.

"Good boy," she whispered.

The thrill of saving the abused dog rushed through her like lightning.

He licked her face, leaving a wet spot on her chin. The cool air tingled against the spot. He was awfully affectionate and friendly for having lived through the abuse he suffered.

"No shelters for you," she murmured making a quick decision. "You're coming home with me and Wiggles until we find someone who can take you in."

He licked her again as she gingerly stepped out of the snowy yard and headed to her car. Opening the back door, she pushed the dog in and wrapped him in the blanket she'd brought.

Not until she was on the highway heading back to her

house did she feel like she had done something wrong. It was then she realized that, after all, she had just stolen someone else's dog. By law, Mutt was the woman's property. Then again, she thought biting her lip, bad laws were meant to be changed.

"Do you want another biscuit?" she asked, digging into her pocket and pulling out another one. Mutt pushed his head between the seats, grabbed it from her hand and disappeared behind the backseat. As she drove on she began to wonder how she was going to explain this new adoptee to Bob. She couldn't tell anyone what she had done. No one would ever understand. Especially Bob.

But, in her heart, Rose was now fully committed to her mission and she knew she was never going to stop.

❖ 🐾 **Chapter 13**

Strange Homecoming

Though she had taken the first momentous step of stealing an animal to save it, the most difficult part, she knew, was going to be telling Bob what she had done. In fact, she told herself nervously, *wait until Bob sees Mutt*. For the next few days, Rose agonized about how to break the news.

Then, on Thursday, the doorbell rang. She froze. Who could that be? Bob? But he had keys. Why would he be ringing the doorbell? The bell rang again.

She shut Wiggles and Mutt in the bedroom and raced to the front door.

She opened it, making sure she didn't let anyone on the other side see into the house, which was a mess.

"I'm lucky you're home." Bob took off his sunglasses, revealing his intense blue eyes. "I forgot my keys to the house and didn't realize it until I got here."

"Hi." Rose covered the doorway, not wanting him to see the state of the house. The only problem, of course, was how she would keep him out. Maybe she could send him on a grocery run. "Could you get some shopping done right now? We're really low on food. We need eggs, milk, bread. The basics."

He eyed her suspiciously. "Why are we always running out of food, Rose? It's just us two and a few pets, isn't it? Besides, I've been on the road for days. I want to relax at home." He stepped toward her, in an effort to move through the doorway, but Rose held her ground.

"Can I come into my own house?" he gruffly asked, pointing at the door behind her.

"We really need groceries, Bob," she insisted. She also needed enough time to figure out what to say to him about the new addition. And the way Bob reacted to chaos, it was not a good idea to let him see Mutt and find out about her new-found project and the fact that she quit her job. Not just yet.

She slipped out to the front step and brought the door closer against her back.

"Why are you acting so strange?" he asked. "And why aren't you at work?"

"I uh... I decided to take the day off."

"Since when do you take a day off?" He peered over her shoulder and through the slight crack in the door. "You don't have someone in there do you?" he finally asked in a very dry tone.

"Now who would I have over?" she defended herself, knowing full well what he was implying. "Really, Bob. How can you think something like that?"

"Why else wouldn't you want me in the house?" he snapped. "Damn it. How could you?" He pushed past her and stormed into the house. "Where's the son of a bitch?" he cried.

Rose winced, dreading Bob's reaction. What would have been worse? Him finding the two dogs, the house empty of food again and her quitting her job because she wanted to rescue dogs or him finding a lover in their house?

"Oh my God, Rose! What the hell happened to the house?" he boomed from the living room. "Where did all these books and newspapers come from?"

Rose sighed and went inside. How was she going to explain that for the last few days she'd done nothing but go through newspaper after newspaper, newsletter after newsletter, flyer after flyer, to find out how to help animals.

"I can't believe this!" He snatched up one of the newsletters from the end table and looked at it. " 'An animal's right to food and shelter,'" he read aloud. He tossed it aside. "I can't believe this. I got a crazy activist on my hands now."

Quickly, he walked toward the bedroom, opened the door and went in. She heard the door slam and his muttering curses as he stormed back out.

"Okay, Rose. There's a brown dog as well as that other one in our bedroom. Do you want to tell me what the hell's going on?"

"Bob, things have been really crazy around here," she calmly tried to explain.

His eyes opened wide as if he'd seen right into her. "Apparently. Well, do you want to tell me what this is all about?"

He walked toward her and stood in the middle of the living room, shaking his head. "Are we starting an animal shelter here in our house?"

She laughed nervously. "Of course not. I just plan on reading about them."

"Rose," he said exasperatedly. "You'd better tell me what's up." He shook his head again, tossed his sunglasses on the coffee table and pushed aside some papers to sit down on the couch.

She sighed, sat down beside him and began to pour out the story of how she'd rescued Mutt.

Throughout Rose's explanation, Bob was silent, just shaking his head back and forth in disbelief. Finally, he said, "I need more stability in my life, Rose. I'm already under pressure trying to start my own company, getting clients, keeping the books, hiring drivers."

Rose took a deep breath and let it out.

"I think it's time you call Rick and ask for a little vacation time. You must be cracking up. Really, Rose, I think you're losing it."

Rose crossed her arms. "Actually, I'm on vacation now, Bob."

"One day isn't what I call a vacation. I mean, not even a week would be enough for you. You're far from just stressed out."

She paused, gulped in some air and stammered, "Well, that is, I am taking more than a day off." She paused to study his face. It looked impatient and uncomprehending, but she had to go on. "I'm taking something more like a sabbatical or rather permanent leave, although my life right now is anything but a vacation."

"You mean you got fired?" he bellowed. "After all you did for that company? Rick fired you? Just like that?"

He got up and began pacing back and forth. "I don't believe it. They fired you, didn't they? What did you do?"

Rose shook her head. "I didn't do anything. And nobody fired me. I quit."

"You what!" Bob came to a stop in front of her and slapped his hand on his forehead. "What do you mean, you quit?"

"Bob, I've found out what I really want to do with my life and it's not working as an accountant. I don't want to be a bean counter for the rest of my days here on earth."

Bob's hand dropped to his side. "And I take it all this stuff around here plus another dog has something to do with what you want to do?"

She sighed and got up, wanting to stand face to face with him. "Yes," she said firmly. "It has everything to do with it."

He waved her away. "Rose, this is serious. We can't support ourselves right now without your job. You know that."

"Just a moment ago you were telling me I worked too much."

"But you're going from one extreme to the other! You need to bring some kind of money in. Margaret and Emily are in college, for crying out loud. We don't even have the house paid off and my new company is only in start-up phase."

He grabbed her hands and looked at them. "And you've been chewing your nails again. Didn't you promise you'd chew gum? Gum is a lot less destructive."

Rose pulled back her hands and stepped away. "There are worse things to do than chew my nails. Bob, for heaven's sake, you're acting like I don't have any control over my life."

"Am I wrong to assume that? Just look at the house!" he cried, waving his hands about. "I don't see what you have under control here. You just quit your job; the house is a mess and we're being overrun by stray animals!"

"I know that it looks like I'm having a mental breakdown, but I'm not. For the first time in my adult life I have a mission I have to complete."

Bob gave her a long pensive look, then began picking up papers. "So you quit your job, let the house go and don't even buy food. Does that sound sane to you?" He began making a neat pile of the papers. "So what are you going to do?" he quietly asked, his head bent over the stack. "I think I have the right to know."

"I'm going to rescue the neglected dogs of Dalton City."

"Wait a minute." He held up his hand. "Rescue dogs?"

"There are hundreds of dogs in Dalton City. Didn't rescuing Wiggles and Hardwin mean anything to you? Didn't Hardwin's suffering and his death mean anything? And I had to save Mutt—he was being tortured."

"Mutt. Is that the new one?" he asked, shaking his head.

"Yes, Bob, and there are so many dogs like Hardwin, Wiggles and Mutt that are neglected or abused and need help. So many it's heartbreaking."

"Don't you realize what you're getting yourself into? You're not some Mother Teresa for dying dogs!" he exclaimed.

She shook her head. "Maybe I shouldn't be telling you this, but just a week before I rescued Mutt, I had another awful experience." She looked away, trying to hide the tears that were surfacing. "I witnessed a guy choking his dog to death. Basically, he killed him, because I tried to help the dog. After that, I knew I had to do something. And when I went back to Dalton City to feed those poor animals, there was this lady shaking Mutt and chaining him to freeze in the snow in order to teach him a lesson. When I saw that I knew what it was I had to do." She took a deep breath, trying not to sound hysterical. "Grandma once told me that there comes a time in every person's life when he or she is presented with the opportunity to better the world. I never believed it, but you know what? My opportunity has finally come. I want to rescue dogs."

Bob cocked his head. "You're serious about this, aren't you?"

Rose took his hands and brought them toward her, trying to reach out to him. "Don't think I'm crazy, Bob. Please don't think I'm crazy. If you knew what I have gone through since you've been gone, you'd understand."

He put his hand on her shoulder. "Look, Rose. I can't stop you from doing what you want to do. But listen to me just this once. Keep it strictly to helping strays. You can't take other people's property, which is what this new dog is. Strays don't belong to anyone. Please."

She half-nodded, knowing she couldn't promise anything.

Bob shook his head and grinned despite himself. "Well, at least now I know where all the food went. Just try to keep food for us humans in the house, will you?"

Rose threw herself into his arms. The pain of what she lived through over the past few weeks seemed to slowly diminish. She knew Bob didn't totally understand that the comfort he was offering was only a beginning, but it meant everything to her.

When Rose walked through the door of her office at ten the next morning, she felt as if everyone was staring at her. She wondered if Rick had told them she was quitting her job to go out and rescue dogs or if she was just being paranoid.

"Hey, stranger. Finally decided to show up at work, huh?" a man remarked, walking by.

"Very funny, Mark. Very funny." She figured she was going to be hearing a lot more jokes.

She walked up to the receptionist's desk. "Is Rick in?" she asked.

Lillian grinned as she stood up. "Taking the day off, Rose?"

"Actually, I've quit."

"Quit?" Lillian stared at Rose as if she didn't understand. "What do you mean, quit?" Lillian asked again. "You mean quit-quit? Or do you mean you're taking a leave of absence?"

Rose shook her head. "Actually, I've quit for good."

"Wow," Lillian gasped. "I had no idea. Have you told Rick?"

"Yes. In fact, I'm here to see him. Is he in?"

"Yes, but he's in a meeting."

"With?"

"Mr. Valerie and some of his people."

"Great. I'm in time then. I have the paperwork for Mr. Valerie's account right here." Rose held up her briefcase.

Lillian shook her head. "I'm not sure Rick would want you going into the meeting after quitting."

"He knows I'm coming in for it," Rose replied, trying not to sound snippy. "I really need to get going. So, if you don't mind, I'd like to be announced."

"But—"

"Lillian, please. I'll never ask another favor of you again. Just do this for me. It'll make my life a whole lot easier."

Lillian nodded and picked up the phone. "Mr. Daniels? Rose is here to see you." She paused. "Yes, Mr. Daniels." She smiled and put the phone down.

"Can I go in?" Rose quickly asked, stepping toward the meeting room.

"Yes. They're expecting you."

"Thanks, Lillian."

"Sure thing. Good luck."

Rose knocked on the closed door that said Conference Room and waited.

"Come in."

Rose quickly walked in and closed the door behind her. "Good morning, everyone."

Rick immediately stood up, his knuckles turning white against the conference table as he leaned on it. *"Rose?"*

The eyes of all the men sitting around the conference table were focused on her. "You're a couple of days late," Rick said frowning.

"I apologize for keeping you all waiting. I have Mr. Valerie's account paperwork right here, all in order." She walked up to the empty chair beside Rick, placed her briefcase on the conference table and opened it.

Pulling out a stack of papers, she laid them out on the table. "I realize I'm leaving at a bad time, but I want you all to know that this is my very best work and I'll be helping Rick make the transition to a new account manager for you."

Rick leaned toward her. "Rose," he whispered, "are you sure?"

"I am, Rick," she said, pressing his hand.

He gave a heavy sigh.

She pointed at the papers and said, "If you have any questions, I'll be glad to answer them."

"Tell me something, Mrs. Block," a deep male voice drawled. Rose knew the voice all too well. It was Mr. Valerie himself.

She usually dreaded talking to the big account, so to speak, but it wasn't like her job was on the line anymore. As she observed the man, she folded her arms in front of her.

"Is Mr. Daniels not paying you enough to stay with my account?" he asked after a momentary pause.

She looked at Rick, confused. He hadn't told Mr. Valerie why she was leaving. Was this idea of quitting her job to rescue dogs so bizarre, so insane? She stared at Rick a moment longer as he tapped his pen against the conference table, then turned to answer Mr. Valerie's question.

She tried to smile, to conceal the way she felt inside.

"I'm sorry. I thought Mr. Daniels would have told you. This isn't about money."

"What then?" Mr. Valerie leaned back into his chair.

"I've decided there are others that need me more."

"Others? Oh, you mean like other accounts?" He laughed. "How can it not be about money, then? It's all about money. Listen, I'll give you more than any of them could offer. You always save my company more money than we know what to do with anyway."

"You don't understand, Mr. Valerie," she gently explained. "I'm leaving the company altogether. I'm planning to rescue abused and neglected dogs."

"Dogs?" Mr. Valerie sat up in his chair, his red tie popping out of his vest. "You mean the 'woof-woof' sort of dogs?"

She tried not to take offense. "Yes. The 'woof-woof' sort, Mr. Valerie."

"You're not serious?"

"Very. I can't turn a blind eye to animal cruelty anymore. And the sooner I leave here, the sooner I can get to my real work."

He stared at her a moment longer then threw back his head and laughed. And it wasn't amused laughter, but something derisive and insulting. His laugh caught on with others in the room. Before long, the only two people left who weren't laughing along were Rose and Rick. *At least my boss doesn't think this is funny,* she thought.

"I'm so sorry you find it amusing," she said over the laughter. "But starving, half dead, disease-ridden, tortured animals aren't funny to me." She slammed her briefcase shut, hoping to silence their monkey-like laughter.

"I'll miss working with you, Rick," she said softly, picking her briefcase up off the table.

With that, she walked out of the conference room. She caught Lillian at the door.

Lillian cracked a guilty smile. "I know I shouldn't have been listening, but with you going away and all, I wanted to know what was going on." She paused. "Anyway, I think you're doing a wonderful thing."

Rose smiled back. "You really think so?" she quietly asked.

"Hey, I have three dogs: Amber, Charlie and Toto." Lillian's face glowed as she mentioned their names. "I adopted them all. I wanted to take in a lot more, but I can't handle any more than three. Anyway, they're all I have and I love them as if they were human."

For the first time since Rose had known Lillian, she felt a deep warmth for her that went beyond the typical friendly feelings she'd had toward her co-workers. It wasn't the fact that Lillian owned dogs. It was the way she glowed when she spoke about them.

"I know what you mean." Rose nodded. "I have to go now, but let's meet for dinner sometime soon, okay?" Rose waved good-bye as she headed for the door.

"So what does your husband think of all this?" Lillian called after her.

At the door, Rose turned around. "Not much. But I'm praying he'll come to understand all of this."

Rose let out a sigh of relief when the door closed behind her. Then, with renewed vigor and a bounce in her step, she headed down the long flight of stairs. She felt better about herself now than she had in a long time. She felt like the old Rose who had cried, "Higher! Higher!" when her grandmother had pushed her on that rickety swing in the yard long ago, when life seemed so simple.

❧ ❧ Chapter 14

Dump Dog Month

Winter was clutching Michigan with its icy hands, and strays in Dalton City were in danger of freezing to death. Rose was going out to feed them all the time now. With Bob frequently on the road, she only had one mission: To help more and more dogs.

Late one Tuesday evening, she turned her van onto a dark street off Fuller, so she could remain undetected by everyone—dogs and people alike. Watching what went on in the neighborhood was the only thing that gave her peace since this was how she could discover which dogs were suffering or being abused.

As she sat in the van watching the desolate street, she noticed a small figure sprinting straight toward her van. As the figure drew closer, she was surprised to find little Mike knocking on her van window.

She unlocked the door, and he slipped in.

"Hi," he said. "Man, it's cold out tonight."

"Mike, what are you doing out this late? Shouldn't you

be sleeping?" she scolded. "How did you know it was me sitting in here anyway?"

He shrugged. "I always look out for your van. I memorized your license plate number. And it's not that late. It's only nine thirty."

"Does your grandma know you're wandering the streets on your own?"

"I told her I was going to see you. She said it was okay."

Rose shook her head. "I haven't seen you for a while. Why haven't you called about any dogs? Haven't you seen any?"

"All the time." He sniffed and wiped his nose into the sleeve of his jacket. "Grandma says not to bother you about them though, unless they're in really bad shape. And I figure now that it's Dump Dog Month, you'll have your hands full."

She stared at him, "Dump Dog Month? What's that?"

"Just like it sounds. People around here dump their dogs in January. I guess after the holidays, people don't have enough money to hold on to them."

"So they dump them?"

"Yep. Right out into the cold. Half of them don't make it, because they don't know how to survive on the street."

She was in awe of the suffering this little boy had seen and felt. "Mike, I am just amazed how much you know."

"Well, I love animals. They don't hurt you like people do."

Rose stared at him wondering what else this child had been through. But she wouldn't ask him. One day, if he felt comfortable, he would tell her.

"You could really help me out," she said.

He shook his head. "Grandma doesn't want me getting too involved. She says I got schoolwork to worry about."

"And she's right," Rose agreed. "But if you ever have any free time and see bad things happening, call me. I can save more dogs with your help."

"Really?"

"Really. And as I showed you earlier, I'm willing to pay

you ten dollars a dog. It's not enough just to feed them, you know. You alerted me to that. There only seem to be more and more of them."

They were quiet for a moment and he shifted in the seat. "You know, this here is the biggest stretch of field you'll ever see in Dalton City." He pointed toward his right. "They took down some buildings last year and never built anything back on it. There are some trees here and there and grass and weeds growing back. It's a nice little place those stray dogs visit when they need to get away from people. Before Grandma took me in I used to go there, too. There's lots of places to hide."

Rose squinted her eyes to better see the vacant lot. Funny. Little Mike referred to it as a field. But she supposed he'd never seen anything but city streets.

"Do you still go out there?"

"Sure do. And if you sit there long enough, you'll see lots of dogs."

She looked over at him and saw Mike staring toward the vacant lot. She leaned against the steering wheel and there they sat in silence for several minutes.

"There's one going over there now," he suddenly whispered. "Just watch."

Rose watched a thin dark shadow cross the road before them and slowly head toward the vacant lot Mike had pointed out. The animal was so feeble and weak it wavered unsteadily as it walked.

"Poor thing," she said. "If we save it, what would you call it?"

He stared at the dog. "We don't even know if it's a boy dog or a girl dog."

"Let's say it's a girl dog."

He thought for a moment. "How about Lucy?"

"Lucy it is. How about we try to rescue her?" she asked, her eyes still watching the lone dog.

"You mean just pick her up?"

She nodded. "Otherwise, she's going to starve to death. Just look at her. She's well on her way. I've got a dog pole in the back and some food. How about you wave the food at her and I use the pole?"

Rose squinted and tried to make out where the dog was heading. Leaning sideways, she tried to see whether it had already disappeared into the dark or if it was still within reach.

"I guess we could get her," Mike said. "When should we do it?"

"How about right now?" Rose grabbed one of the many plastic bags full of dog food she had earlier prepared and handed it to Mike. "Open the bag, go over there and toss it to her. I have a cage in back. Once you get her interest, I'll head around and try to trap her."

Little Mike climbed out of the van and followed Rose's instructions. Within moments, he had the dog edging closer and closer to his outstretched hand.

Rose grabbed for the dog pole and got out of the van as quietly as possible. She crept over to the field, undetected by the dog who was busy trying to build up enough confidence in Mike to take the food from him. Rose got a good look at the dog and winced at what appeared to be a painful injury. Her ear looked like it had been torn off. Her heart racing, Rose pushed out the pole as far as she could and, sensing it was around the dog's neck, tightened it.

The dog started barking, disrupting the quiet night, but as Rose pulled the dog closer and closer to the van, little Mike was right there by her side, waving the food as a gesture of comfort.

"It's all right," Rose gently reassured the dog. "It's all right."

The dog finally stopped barking and instead anxiously stared up at them.

Within moments, the dog was in the car. Surprisingly, the tension left the animal and it wagged its tail. It was now calm and friendly enough that she didn't even need to cage it. "And wouldn't you know," Rose said as she examined the dog, "It's a girl." Mike's name fit.

"Give Lucy the whole bag of food," she told him.

The dog wolfed down every bit.

"So what are you going to do with her?" Mike asked, turning to the backseat and giving Lucy a pat.

"I'm going to keep her until I can find her a good home. And speaking of home, that's where you should be heading." She picked up her purse and yanked out her wallet. Retrieving a ten-dollar bill, she gave it to him. "That's for helping me out."

He looked at the money in his hand then grinned. "Thanks."

"I'll drop you off at your house and we'll call it a night," she said suddenly weary.

Mike nodded, and within moments they were in front of his grandmother's home. Before he got out, Mike opened up another plastic bag of dog food that Lucy was sniffing and let her eat more.

He then quickly slipped out of the car so that the dog wouldn't have a chance to follow him and escape. He waved as he climbed the front steps then disappeared into his house.

Rose looked into the backseat of her van where Lucy was devouring her second portion of dog food. "It's just you and me, Lucy," she commented. "I'll take you to the clinic for that ear and then we'll go home."

❧ ❧ Chapter 15

Hearts, Flowers and a Black Dog

Valentine's Day. Rose had always loved the holiday and this year she was lucky. She wasn't going to be spending it alone. Not only her daughters, but Bob would be with her. She was in the kitchen, putting the finishing touches on dinner when her daughters arrived.

"Hi, Mom!" Margaret cried, coming through the door and giving her a hug.

"Hi, Mom!" Emily called, coming in right after her. "So, where's Bob? Did he make it home yet?"

Rose withheld a smile. "No. Not yet. But he'll be here soon." She was just as excited as they were that they would be spending Valentine's Day together without Bob being on the road.

Three simultaneous friendly barks interrupted their conversation.

"Mom, you have three dogs now?" Emily asked, falling to her knees as the dogs charged into the room. She lovingly rubbed Lucy's large head, then Wiggles' still growing hair and lastly Mutt's. "They're all so beautiful. What does Bob think?"

"Bob doesn't know about Lucy yet. He's been gone for two weeks, so I haven't had the chance to tell him."

Emily looked up at her, raising an eyebrow. "I hope he doesn't freak out."

"I'm crossing my fingers. Lucy's got nowhere to go. She's too old to be adopted."

Rose heard someone fiddling with the front door lock and felt her heart jump. *Here's hoping that Valentine's Day will soften Bob's heart into letting me keep Lucy*, she thought.

"Hey, it's him!" Emily cried, popping up.

Rose waved a hand at her. "Take the dogs upstairs so they're out of sight," she said hurriedly.

Margaret and Emily quickly ushered the dogs out of the room and up the stairs as the front door opened and closed.

Bob, dressed in a gray pinstriped suit, walked into the kitchen. A red rose stuck out of his fisted hand. He looked as stiff as a piece of cardboard.

Rose laughed. "Hello, stranger. Where'd you steal the suit from?"

"What?" He looked down at himself. "You don't like it? I got it when I was on the road. I thought I'd impress you."

She shook her head. "You look great. I just thought I'd never see you in a suit. And with a rose, too."

He pushed the flower toward her and gave her a hurried kiss on the cheek. "Good to see you."

"Good to see you, too." She took the rose and lifted the petaled bloom to her nose. "This is lovely," she uttered breathing in the fragrance. She couldn't remember the last time Bob had given her flowers.

"Hey, Bob," Margaret and Emily chimed together as they rushed down the stairs and into the kitchen.

Long overdue kisses and hugs were exchanged.

"Why don't you guys sit down at the table?" Rose quickly headed toward the dining room. "I'll start bringing the food in." Bob and the girls followed.

Bob rounded the table set with Rose's best white lace

Here are photographs of some of the many dogs Rose Block has rescued from both the streets and abusive owners. For the protection of the dogs and Rose, names have been withheld and some details altered.

Rose found these two siblings as malnourished puppies wandering the streets with their sick mother. Though the puppies were quickly treated and adopted, their mother had such an extreme case of heartworm she was not expected to survive. Finally, after more than a year of medical treatment the puppies' mother miraculously survived.

This terribly abused dog was petrified of men but not aggressive toward Rose when she rescued him. Though he doesn't fear women, today, the only person he truly trusts is Rose.

Rose found this shih tzu on the side of the road sick and injured. With medicine, care and love, Rose nursed the little dog back to health.

Malnourished and heartworm positive when she found him, Rose took this fluffy, white dog in and he's been a part of her animal family ever since.

When Rose rescued this German shepherd mix, he was underweight, heartworm positive and had mange and other illnesses. Once she got him treatment, Rose placed the dog with a loving couple.

Scared, sick and with a broken leg when Rose found her, this black corgi/shepherd mix was treated and became a permanent member of the family.

After witnessing this dog being mistreated by its owner, Rose rescued him. She soon learned the animal suffered serious brain damage from abuse which caused dangerous and uncontrollable behavior. With no treatment options available, the dog had to be put down.

Being starved and abused was no life for this little dog. After rescuing her, Rose placed the puppy in a good home.

One of a litter of abandoned puppies found and rescued by Rose, this dog and all her siblings were adopted.

Rose found this black and tan dog wandering the streets near her home, sick and weak from hunger. After medical treatment and spaying, she was placed in a wonderful home with two children and lives happily ever after.

tablecloth and china, and looking anxious, sat down. Margaret and Emily took their places as Rose went back into the kitchen, pulled on her oven mitts and opened the oven door to make sure the homemade vegetable lasagna was done. Bubbling sauce and melted cheese told her it was ready to come out of the oven.

Emily came into the room and stood next to her. "Mom?"

Rose pulled out the large baking dish that held the lasagna and hefted it to the top of the stove. "Yes, sweetie?"

"You should probably tell Bob about the dog," she whispered. "You know how he is about surprises. Especially surprises he doesn't like."

Rose took the loaf of garlic bread she'd been heating out of the oven and placed it on the cutting board. With a bread knife, she carefully cut the loaf into several pieces and arranged them neatly in a breadbasket, placing a napkin over top to help keep the bread warm. "He'll find out soon enough as well as the fact that the clinic charged me two hundred dollars for everything. Now, could you grab the salad and the bread? We'd better get back in there and try to distract him." She put a trivet under her arm and picked up the baking dish.

Rose hurriedly headed out of the kitchen, the lasagna weighing heavily in her arms, but not as heavily as her thoughts. Emily followed carrying a mixed green salad and the breadbasket.

Rose felt badly about keeping Lucy a secret, but she knew Bob wouldn't take the news of another dog living with them well. Or the fact that the dog had been taken from Dalton City, where he didn't want her to go. And not only that, but it would be obvious to Bob that Lucy wasn't going to be the last dog she'd bring into the house.

Rose had decided that feeding the Dalton City strays wasn't enough. She had to start taking them off the street, one by one, and if some of the dogs needed to stay in their house, then stay they would.

"That looks great, Mom," Margaret said.

"Sure does," Emily and Bob echoed.

It was quiet at the table for a time as everyone stared at the harvest of food before them.

The silence was suddenly interrupted when Lucy, Mutt and Wiggles started barking, asking to join the feast.

"Let them come down, Emily," Rose said with a sigh.

"Sure thing." Emily scurried upstairs. Soon, all three dogs joined them.

Bob leaned back in his chair, a surprised look on his face. "What's this?" He pointed at Lucy as she bounded into the room followed by Mutt, Wiggles and Emily.

Rose quickly tore a slice of bread into several pieces and put them on a plate which she set in the corner of the room for the dogs. Lucy, Mutt and Wiggles rushed over to devour the treat.

"Let's say a prayer," Margaret offered, when Rose sat down again.

Margaret folded her hands. "Thank you, dear Lord, for all that you have given our family. We are truly blessed to be spending this time together." She paused. "Also bless Lucy, Mutt and Wiggles who Mom, with her soft heart, rescued from the street against Bob's will. And may Mom stay out of further trouble."

"Margaret!" Rose cried, glaring at her.

"Amen," Margaret finished with a smile.

"Amen," Emily joined in.

Rose worriedly looked over at Bob. He was still leaning back in his chair watching Lucy.

"So where'd you get him?" he asked, looking over at her.

"It's a she."

"So where'd you get *her*?" he insisted.

"I found her." She stood up, cut a large piece of the vegetable lasagna and scooped it onto Emily's plate.

"Where?"

"Oh, uh, not too far from here." She tried not to look at him, for fear that the guilt she felt would somehow show.

"And how are the cats taking this?" he asked. "Being outnumbered and all."

"Oh, they're getting used to it."

"Right. So where did you really get this dog, Rose?"

It was quiet for a moment.

"Dalton City, right? Why the hell do you keep going back into that neighborhood?" he finally asked. "Didn't I ask you to stay out of there?"

Rose frantically cut another huge portion of lasagna and piled it onto Margaret's plate.

"That's more than enough, Mom," Margaret commented, holding her hands up to signal that she didn't want any more.

Rose, hands shaking, grabbed the breadbasket and passed it to Margaret. Then she heaped a piece of lasagna onto a plate and placed it in front of Bob.

"Mom, are you alright?" Emily asked.

It seemed like the attacks were coming at Rose from all sides. She felt trapped and wished she could run away. Suddenly, she took the spatula she was using to serve the lasagna and slapped it down hard on her plate. The sharp sound made everyone at the table flinch. "Everyone, just eat," Rose ordered, unable to conceal her agitation. Her command was followed by stunned silence.

Ignoring the stares of her family, Rose scooped up lasagna from the baking dish for herself. With shaky hands, she was relieved to get the pasta to her plate without dropping it. Then she noticed sauce and cheese dripping over the edge of her plate onto the tablecloth. She swore silently and used her napkin to dab at the stain.

Bob finally broke the silence. "You didn't answer my question, Rose."

"Your question? What was your question?"

"Come on, Rose. You know what I'm talking about. What is it with you and Dalton City?"

"I can't turn my back on that place, okay?" she cried. "There are too many dogs out there and January was officially Dump Dog Month, when people abandon their dogs, because they feel they can't afford their Christmas bills and a dog. Now, if you don't mind, I'm hungry and I'd like to eat."

She cut a large piece of lasagna and stabbed at it with

her fork. Pushing it into her mouth, she began slowly chewing. With her mouth full of food, she wouldn't have to answer any more questions.

Bob, on the other hand, wasn't eating. He stared at her, making her feel like a criminal under scrutiny. "When is this going to stop?"

Rose was beginning to wonder whether this family dinner was such a good idea. The food didn't even taste that good to her and the conversation? Even her girls weren't supporting her.

"You can't save every abandoned or abused dog there is, you know. Half of them are gonna die whether you like it or not."

She swallowed another piece of pasta then slammed her fork onto the plate. "I'm trying to eat."

Bob looked down at his plate and turned it one way then the other. "I can't keep going on the road not knowing if I'm coming home to another dog."

"And why can't you?" she cried, standing up. "You're never around! Does it matter if you have to look at them for half a day before you go back out on the road? I need them as much as they need me, do you understand?"

"Mom, please," Margaret said, wiping her mouth. "Be nice. It's the first time we've had a meal together in a long time. Don't ruin it."

"Be nice? Be nice?" Rose cried, her voice getting shrill. "He's giving me the third degree and then says 'They're gonna die anyway.' Does that sound *nice* to you? I've never met anyone more selfish in my entire life and I—"

"Mom, really. I don't think that you're being—"

The telephone interrupted Margaret's words.

Rose took in a shaky breath and gratefully went off to answer it.

Another minute at the table and she would have started crying. Couldn't Bob just leave the matter about the dogs alone? Lucy, Mutt and Wiggles were hers and that was that.

She picked up the phone. "Yes, hello?"

"Hey, is this Doggy Pickup?"

She raised a brow. "Doggy Pickup?" she repeated.

"Yeah, I was looking for the lady that picks up the dogs. I can't remember her name. But she gave me this number."

"Who is this?"

"Royce, the guy who told you about the dog the guy was beating up."

"Royce? Oh, yes, of course! *Royce.*" The homeless man. She hurried into her bedroom with the cordless phone and closed the door behind her. "Yes, hi, Royce. It's me, Rose."

"Oh yeah, that's right. Rose. I couldn't remember your name. Anyway, I'm calling about a dog. A female dog. It's not doing too good. It can't seem to move around. I think she's got a broken leg and with things being so cold, I don't think she'll make it."

"Okay." Rose ran a shaky hand through her hair, trying to calm herself. "And where is she now?"

"About a block from where you took that light brown one."

She was quiet for a moment. "I don't know what you mean."

"You took that dog the man was beating on, didn't you? He ain't in that yard anymore. Unless he died or something."

Rose swallowed hard and closed her eyes, trying not to think about the horrible night she witnessed murder. "What about this dog you're calling about now, Royce?"

"Oh yeah. Right. She's hiding in the bushes of twenty-three sixty-three on Fifth. I made sure I got the house number for you."

"Twenty-three sixty-three on Fifth. And you said she's got a broken leg?"

"Yeah and she's real skinny, too. I don't think she's had nothing to eat in a real long time. It's not like she can go anywhere to get food. She's been stuck in those bushes."

She sighed. "Okay. How about you meet me there in an hour?"

"It's ten dollars for the dog, right?"

She smiled. "Yes. Ten dollars."

"Okay then. See you there in an hour."

"Thanks for calling, Royce. It means a lot to me."

He laughed. "Yeah. It means a lot to me, too. I need the money."

She hesitated. "Royce, uh, are you hungry at all? I mean it's Valentine's Day and I made a big dinner. I can bring some food if you want."

"I wouldn't mind something."

Rose nodded. "Good."

"Food and the ten dollars, right?"

"Food and the ten dollars."

"Great. See you soon then."

Rose set down the phone. She would have to make an excuse to get away without telling the girls or Bob where she was going. As if things weren't already bad enough. She only hoped when she came back from Dalton City that Bob would already be in bed and the girls back to their college dorms.

She hurried back into the dining room.

Everyone was still quietly eating. Everyone, that is, except Bob. He continued to stare at his untouched plate, tapping his fork against it.

"Bob, you should eat something," she murmured, picking up a plate and putting as much food as she could onto it.

"I'm not hungry."

She continued piling lasagna on the plate, making sure no sauce or cheese spilled over the sides. She grabbed a few slices of garlic bread and placed them on top.

"Are you going to eat all that?" Emily asked, holding a fork in midair, her eyes on the plate Rose was holding.

"No, of course not. I'm taking this to a friend."

"A human friend or a dog friend?" Margaret asked. "You're not going out, are you? It's late."

"I'll be back as soon as I can." She headed to the kitchen to get some aluminum foil and wrapped the plate tightly. Then she searched through a drawer until she found some plastic utensils.

Emily followed her. "Mom, you can't go. We haven't had a family dinner. Besides, we have cards and candy for you."

"I'm sorry, Emily. I want to stay, but I just can't," Rose said. She put on her coat and headed for the front door, balancing the plate on the palm of her hand. "Save some cherry pie for me, will you?"

Bob got up and hurried after her. "Tell me where you're going?"

"Not far." She tried not to look at him as she shoved each foot into her boots. She opened the door and called, "I'll be back soon," before slamming it closed behind her.

Thirty minutes later, she was in Dalton City. Royce was already waiting on Fifth. Parking and getting out of her van, she hurried toward him handing him the utensils and the plate. "The food's still warm. And don't worry about the plate. You can keep it."

She dug into her coat pocket and pulled out a ten-dollar bill. "And this is for you, too."

Royce shifted the plate beneath his arm and took the money. "Thanks. You gonna take her?"

"If she lets me."

"She's right over there near the bushes." He pointed. "She'll let you take her. She don't have anywhere else to go. Well, I gotta go. Thanks." He bobbed a good-bye and headed off, disappearing behind an abandoned house.

Rose looked toward the small clump of bushes and tried to make out the dog within them. A low whimper came from the brush. It was clear the dog was hiding and didn't want to be disturbed. This was going to require a leash.

She headed back to the van and yanked out one of the leashes she had bought at PetSmart. Loosening the loop, she tested it to make sure it would tighten. Now she needed something with which to lure the dog. Food. She needed food.

She pulled out a plastic bin from beneath one of the seats and snatched up a can of dog food. Popping it open, she put the lid into a plastic bag and headed back to where the dog was.

"Hey," she gently called, rounding the bushes. "I've got something for you."

Rose edged closer and closer, holding out the can of dog food with one hand and clutching the trapping leash with the other. If Royce was right about the broken leg, then it shouldn't be too hard to catch her. Taking her to the car, on the other hand, was going to be tough.

The whimper turned into a bark as Rose drew closer. She froze and crouched low, peering into the dark bushes. If it weren't so dark, it would have been a lot easier.

"Hello," she gently called again. "Look what I have."

She held out the open can of dog food, hoping the creature had enough strength to care. It was now quiet in the bushes.

"Come on," she prompted, slowly waving the can. "Come on out and get it."

It was quiet for a moment longer and then she heard a shuffle, as if the dog were dragging a weight. A black dog slowly appeared in the dim light of the street lamp.

The dog hesitated, observing Rose with large eyes.

"Come on, sweetie. I'm not going to hurt you." She held the open can of food out for the dog.

It sniffed the air and then moved toward her completely revealing itself for the first time. Rose held back a heart-breaking sob as the dog dragged herself toward Rose using only her front paws. Her hind legs laid out flat behind her, appearing crushed as if a car had driven over them. The dog dragged herself closer and closer, each movement clearly painful to her, until she was within arm's distance sniffing the air again.

Rose held out the can and waited.

The dog hesitated and then as she stuck her furry head out to reach the can of food, Rose skipped the leash around the dog's neck.

The dog reared back as best it could in its instinct to escape, but in the process tightened the leash.

"I'm going to try to carry you. Let's get you to the car as best we can." She yanked on the leash.

The black dog resisted and tried to get back into the bushes.

"Maybe you should eat first." Rose placed the can beneath the dog's muzzle.

The hurt dog lunged at the container and swallowed the

food within moments. Then she knocked over the can looking for more.

"Come with me and you'll get more," Rose said, yanking on the leash. "Come on."

The dog cooperated this time, dragging itself completely out of the bushes and onto the sidewalk. Rose patiently waited as the black dog pulled itself along toward her car. She wanted so much to carry the animal but was afraid to touch its hind legs knowing how painful that would be.

Opening the side door of the van, Rose released the latch on the cage door. She tightly held the leash as she pulled out another can of food and popped the lid off. She strategically placed it in the rear of the cage.

"Okay, sweetie, in you go." Rose swung a leg over the dog and lifted it, making sure not to touch its rear.

The dog's front legs scrambled against her and it began whimpering, but Rose was somehow able to slowly push the scrawny animal into the cage.

Securing the latch, she sighed. It was a good thing Royce had called. It couldn't have lived much longer with these injuries out in the freezing cold. She shut the side door of the van, looked around, then headed toward the emergency clinic. It was probably going to cost her another few hundred dollars. She bit her lip hard.

Home again, Rose parked the van at the curb, picked up her purse and headed for the front door. She felt good, knowing the dog was going to survive. Its hind legs were broken but repairable and, except for malnutrition, very little else was wrong with her.

The front door opened just as Rose was about to stick her key into the lock. It was Bob.

He stepped aside, gesturing for her to come in. She hesitated, noting the angry look on his face, but entered. He slammed the door hard behind them, making her jump.

"Three dogs, a phone call and a grand disappearance for five hours on Valentine's night!" he cried, stepping in front of her. "What the hell is going on with you? Don't you care about your family?"

"Of course I care. I care very much but—"

Lucy, Mutt and Wiggles rushed over, jumping on Rose, whining for attention. She dropped to her knees, thankful for an excuse to avoid Bob's interrogation of her and cuddled the three dogs.

"Rose, you've been blowing a lot of money lately. I don't think I have to tell you what that's doing to us, seeing as you don't have a job."

"What do you mean?" she quietly asked.

"I opened the credit card statement that was sitting out with the rest of the mail. Three thousand dollars. PetSmart, PetSmart, PetSmart and animal clinic after animal clinic are more or less all that's listed. Do you want to explain this to me? Do you want to tell me why all this money is being spent?"

Rose looked up at him, her fingers still working Lucy's soft fur. "I'm going to use what's left of my Christmas bonus to pay for it," she calmly explained. "As for the rest, I'll have to pay the credit card company a little at a time. I'll sell that property on the lake I inherited, if I have to."

"We planned to retire on that property," he reminded her. "And the way you're spending money, selling everything we own is going to be your only choice."

"What do you want me to do, Bob? Who else is going to pay for these dogs?"

He threw his hands up in the air. "Don't you care that I'll work for the rest of my days to pay off credit card bills for dogs that don't even belong to us?"

"Of course I care, but money isn't everything." She turned away. "Look, Bob, I'm so tired. I want to go to bed."

"I'm tired, too, you know that? Dead tired." He dropped to his knees and stared at her. "What's all the money going for? Tell me Rose."

The hostile, silent air between them seemed to tremble. Finally she said, "I feed them all the time and buy supplies that help me help them."

"They're just dogs, Rose." He leaned closer. "Don't you understand?"

Rose concentrated her attention on Wiggles who was still licking her hands. Wiggles suddenly scampered away and settled under the coffee table, leaving her and Bob alone there on the floor.

"Rose? Rose, you're not listening to me. They're just dogs," he repeated.

"For goodness sake, Bob, stop it," she snapped, getting up. "I've tried explaining how I feel to you. And you just don't seem to understand."

He stood up and drew closer, deliberately meeting her eyes. "To tell you the truth," he whispered, "I ought to walk out the door right now, but I love you too much and I just can't."

His hand reached out, possessively cupping the back of her neck and he pulled her hard against him. His lips brushed hers for the first time in weeks.

Rose kissed him back passionately, but felt the need to pull away. She didn't want him to think a kiss would solve their problems. "I'm sorry you feel the way you do, but I'm not going to stop. I can't," she murmured.

His blond brows came together as they always did when he was upset. "Tell me what's going on."

"I told you."

"But why the dogs?"

"Because they are dogs and nobody else seems to give a damn about them. That's why."

"Okay, fine. If you don't want to talk, I'm going to bed. I'm exhausted." He got up and walked around her.

"No, don't go," she pleaded, trailing after him. She missed having him around. "We haven't been together in a long time."

Bob turned around and looked at her with a coolness that chilled her. "What's your idea of being together? I want to know."

The question made her turn pale and her stomach flip-flopped, torturing her soul. "What do you mean?" she softly asked, surprised she had the strength to speak.

"I don't think I have to rephrase it for you. Why are these dogs more important than our marriage?"

"They're not more important, but, Bob, they are important. Don't you understand what I've been saying to you? I wish you could help me. Why do I have to depend on people like Royce and Mike?"

He stared at her. "Royce and Mike? Who the hell are they?"

She reddened. They had grown so far apart. What was happening to her? Why did she feel she couldn't trust anyone, not even Bob? She owed him some form of explanation for what she'd been doing. He was her husband.

"So who the hell are these guys? Is this what you've been doing with your spare time, seeing some guys?"

She laughed despite herself. "Royce is an old homeless man I befriended on my feeding route. He's the guy I dropped the food off for tonight. And Mike is only ten years old. He knows everything about what's going on in the neighborhood. They both keep me informed about dogs in Dalton City that need my help. That way, I don't lose any more."

"So how much are you paying this guy and kid? They're not doing it for free, are they? I mean, one's homeless and the other one's ten years old."

Rose flinched and went on. "I pay them ten dollars for every dog they tell me about."

"Ten dollars a dog? Ten damn dollars a dog!" He threw his hands in the air. "Hell, at ten dollars a dog they'll be stealing dogs from people. Have you lost your mind? Have you—" He shook his head as he backed away. "The next thing you'll be telling me is that you use the van like some dogmobile!"

Rose bit her lip. *Guilty as charged.*

He stared at her. "Damn it, Rose! What aren't you willing to do for these—these dogs?" He approached her and pointed his finger at her. "You're out of a job and I'm struggling to start my business. I don't think I need to remind you we should be saving money, not blowing it on—on starving dogs! There are plenty of organizations to help you out with those strays. This whole room is full of pamphlets and newspapers and flyers proving that."

"I have to find the right ones. A lot of those places end up killing the dogs that are brought in," she tried explaining.

"Don't play with these dogs' lives! They're not a bunch of stuffed animals you can toss into the back of your van!"

A bark and a low growl escaped the dogs as they scrambled to get between them.

"You're upsetting them," Rose said, stepping away from him. She was shaking.

"No, I don't think I'm upsetting them," he dryly said. "I think I'm upsetting you. I want you to tell me right now how many dogs you've fed in the past week. And tell me the truth."

"I don't count," she lied.

"Rose, I can't help you if you shut me out like this."

"I'm not shutting you out. I'm just afraid to let you in."

He glared at her. "I didn't realize I mean that little to you."

She heard the hurt in his voice and wanted to cry. "Bob," she softly pleaded. "Please understand."

"You listen to me, Rose. I'm ordering you to stop. It's them or me."

"Then leave!" she exclaimed, pointing at the door. "Go ahead. Get a hotel room if that's what you want. You're leaving me to go back on the road tomorrow anyway. Go!"

"Fine. Instead of tomorrow, I'll go right now." He headed out the door and slammed it behind him.

✿ ✿ Chapter 16

Lost Valentine

Rose stood in the kitchen watching Lucy, whose ear was still bandaged. The dog strode toward Mutt and nuzzled him. Rose sighed as she filled the kettle with water and put it on the stove to make some tea.

Ever since Bob had walked out on her that night, she felt more alone than she ever had, even with Wiggles, Mutt and Lucy around. She looked at the phone beside the couch and wondered whether she should try calling him on his cell phone.

Suddenly, the phone rang and her heart lurched at the sound. She grabbed the receiver. "Hello?"

It was only the clinic, advising her the dog she'd rescued Valentine's night could be picked up. She told them she'd come right away. After hanging up the phone, she turned off the stove, put on her coat, grabbed her keys and left.

A short while later, the black dog stared at her from the backseat of her van with large brown eyes that pleaded with her for a home—her home.

"I can't," she said, shaking her head. "Bob's been at a

hotel since our scene on Valentine's Day. He called me this morning from the road to say he'd be home. Even if he comes back, I'm going to have to tell him that I spent three hundred dollars to get your back legs fixed, on top of everything else."

The dog lowered her head and rested it on the seat, looking all the more pitiful.

"I did some looking around, though, and I found you a great shelter a few miles from here. You'll be just fine there." Although she spoke soothingly to the dog, she wondered who she was trying to convince more: the dog or herself.

The dog shut her eyes, appearing to drift off to sleep.

Rose sighed and reassured herself that she was doing the right thing taking this animal to a shelter. Wiggles and Mutt she had to keep. Lucy was too old for the shelters, but this dog was still young enough to be wanted. She prayed this new shelter would take her in.

Flakes of snow drifted down from the sky and landed on the windshield. The snow season was still in progress in the third week of February and would probably continue for weeks to come.

Rose slowly pulled out of the clinic parking lot.

With the dog asleep, the van was quiet and she used the silence to try to come up with a good name for the dog. What name was good enough for such a beautiful animal?

As she glanced back at the dog through the rearview mirror, the blackness of its coat reminded her of a past she didn't want to remember and the kitten she had taken in from the cold during her punishments in the basement of the orphanage. Its fur had been the same bright, shiny black as this dog's.

That stray cat had been her only friend. Perhaps that was why she was so intent on saving these dogs—because she remembered how she and that kitten were treated.

At the shelter, Rose slowly led the dog inside, holding on to the collar the clinic had put around her neck. She would have carried her but worried about dropping her on the slippery sidewalk.

Surprisingly, the dog managed to hobble on her two front legs. In the reception area, Rose made sure the dog lay down next to a row of empty chairs alongside the wall. "I'm just going to fill out some papers. You be good."

Rose hurried over to the desk where a thin man with horn-rimmed glasses sat organizing papers. The man's eyes were on the dog the whole time.

"Hi," she said. "I called a few days ago about bringing in a dog."

The man finally stopped staring at the dog and looked at Rose. "Is that the dog right there?" he asked.

Rose nodded, uncertain as to what he was implying.

"What happened to its legs?"

"I don't know," she said. "They were broken when I found her and needed to be put into casts. Is, uh, that a problem?"

The man pulled a framed piece of bright blue paper with large type on it from behind the counter and put it down for Rose to see.

"This is our policy," he said pointing at it.

NOTICE: NO ANIMAL WITH
EXTENSIVE INJURIES WILL BE
KEPT WITHOUT TERMINATION.

"It's usually posted on the wall," he continued while Rose stared at the words, "but it fell down the other day and I keep forgetting to bring a hammer and some nails to put it back up."

Rose finally looked up at the man. "No one told me about this when I called. And I told the woman I talked to on the phone that the dog had two broken legs. She said it wasn't a problem."

"Whoever it is you talked to," the man insisted, "probably thought you were bringing in the dog to have it terminated."

"But I made it clear that I wanted this dog adopted."

He shook his head and leaned on the counter so that he could look Rose in the eye. "It's very hard to adopt out injured animals. Everyone wants healthy ones. People want pets that are easy to maintain."

"She's fine otherwise," Rose pointed out, waving a hand toward the black dog. "The doctor at the emergency clinic assured me of that."

"Regardless, the dog may never walk properly after the casts are removed. It'd be like having a cripple. Like I said, people that come in here looking for dogs want something that is easy to take care of."

Rose worriedly looked at the dog, knowing that its condition was probably going to keep it from being taken by other shelters as well. "What if—what if I kept her until she was healthy again?" she finally asked.

"Then we would take her. I'd say she looks about a year old. So she's not too old to be adopted. Is she trained?"

"Trained?" Rose repeated.

The man nodded.

"She's been out on the street most of her life."

"Well, my advice to you is to keep her until the casts come off. Then train her and bring her back and we'll happily take her. She's beautiful. Anyone would love to have her."

"But not like this," Rose said softly.

"No, not like this."

Rose sighed and wondered what she was going to do. She was sure Bob would leave her permanently if she brought another dog into the house. But what choice did she have? She'd have to explain to him that it would only be for a short time. Until the casts came off.

"Can you help me get her back into the car without having her walk again?"

He nodded, adjusting his glasses. "I'll get one of the guys in the back to help you."

Wiggles, Mutt and Lucy were quick to greet their new sibling. The new dog didn't care for them as much, perhaps thinking they were too hyperactive, and spent most of her time sleeping against the refrigerator door.

Of all the days that Rose could bring home another dog, today was the worst, what with Bob coming home for the first time since their Valentine's Day fight.

After she finished feeding all the dogs, she sat down on the couch in the living room and waited for him to arrive. Over and over in her mind she thought of what she was going to say.

The next thing she knew, Bob was walking through the door.

He smiled at her. Although she smiled back, she felt herself trembling.

"It's snowing outside," he commented, closing the door behind him.

She nodded. "I know."

"It's been a rough winter," he added, stomping the snow off his shoes. He stared at her for a long moment.

"You have that sort of secretive look again," he said. "Did you save another dog?" he asked, making his way toward her.

"Well, I... I just remembered something," she said softly, standing up.

Bob put an arm around her, hugging her close. "What did you remember?"

"When I was in the orphanage, I found a black kitten and named it Valentine."

"What made you think of that?"

Taking a deep breath and letting it out slowly, she tried to state everything as calmly as possible. She began to tell Bob of the small black dog with two broken legs whom she wanted to name Valentine. "The shelter was ready to terminate it and—"

"Are you telling me we have another dog?" he quietly asked. "I mean, you wouldn't name a dog unless—" He drew away.

"Bob, please don't get upset," she quickly said. "She's only staying with us a short while. I promise. She's got two broken legs and the shelter won't take her."

"And I'm assuming we paid for the casts."

She didn't say anything.

He sighed. "Fine, fine. As long as we're not keeping the dog. Name him whatever you want but you'd better promise me right now that he'll be out of here by Easter."

She grinned. "It's a she, Bob."

"Whatever." He stepped away from her. "I need to get something to eat."

Rose continued grinning as he disappeared into the kitchen. And she thought he was going to give her hell. It would seem she didn't know her husband as well as she thought she did.

Bob's head suddenly reappeared from the kitchen doorway. "Valentine is parked right in front of the fridge, Rose. What do you want me to do?"

"Just slowly open the door. She usually scoots away far enough to let you get in. I don't know why she likes being in close to the fridge so much, she just does."

"Great," he called, disappearing again. "Let's just hope these dogs don't learn how to open the damn thing or we'll be the ones starving."

Rose broke out laughing. It wasn't until later that night that she realized Bob had made her laugh for the first time in a very long while.

❧ 🐾 Chapter 17

Just Another Dog

The phone rang. Rose woke up on the sofa with a start. *I must have fallen asleep.* The phone rang again. She stumbled into the kitchen to answer it and looked at the clock. It was almost eleven. Who could be calling so late?

"Hello?"

"Hey," a boyish voice whispered. "It's me."

It took her a moment to realize who it was. "Mike? Mike, are you okay?"

"I didn't mean to call so late," he went on, still whispering, "but Grandma wouldn't let me call you, so I had to wait until she went to bed."

"Mike, I don't want you doing any of this stuff behind your grandmother's back."

"She just worries too much, that's all."

"So why are you calling?" she gently asked.

"Mrs. Green got another dog," he whispered. "I think we should get it from her."

"Who's Mrs. Green?" she asked.

"The woman you took Mutt from."

Rose's heart pounded. "That horrible woman got herself another dog?" It had hardly been a month since she had taken Mutt and the woman already had another dog? Rose shook her head. "I can't just go and take it from her, Mike. She'll probably be waiting for me this time with the police."

"Nuh uh. Today's Friday."

"And what's so special about Friday?"

"She goes out to the bar down the street every Friday. She doesn't come home until after midnight, usually around one in the morning."

Rose laughed. "Mike, how did you become the neighborhood spy at only ten years old?"

"I just see what goes on and I have a real good memory, that's all."

"I could get into a lot of trouble if she catches me. What I did before was for Mutt and Mutt alone."

"She hit this dog in the head with a pot today. I saw it. The dog fell over."

"Oh my God. Did the dog pass out?"

"Yeah, I think so. And then Mrs. Green did something to her neck."

"Her neck?" Rose tensed.

"She chained the dog up by the neck. She pulled the chain so tight it cut the dog's neck real bad. It was bleeding and everything."

Rose closed her eyes in disbelief. "You saw her do that, Mike?"

"Yep. Me and my friend Kevin saw it. She did it Monday afternoon. I yelled at her to stop, but she told me to shut up. She said she did it because the dog was chewing on her shoes."

Rose looked at the kitchen clock again. Just after eleven. She could leave within ten minutes and be there well before midnight. And, since it had been raining for the past few hours, the weather was certain to keep people off the streets and afford her the chance to get the dog without being seen. "Is the dog big?"

"Nope. It looks like it's still a puppy. It maybe comes up to my knees. Oh, hold on, I think Grandma heard me."

There was a shuffle and Rose was sure that he had covered the mouthpiece to prevent her hearing what was said. A few moments later, he came back on. "I gotta go."

"Do you know if Mrs. Green put the dog outside?"

"She always does when she leaves the house. She doesn't trust the dog in the house. Same as with Mutt."

"Thanks for calling, Mike. You've got ten dollars coming to you for this one."

"That's okay. You don't have to pay me for this one. I hate that lady. She's so mean to everyone."

Rose put the phone down on the kitchen table and took a deep breath. That woman treated her dog so horribly. What prevented her from taking the next step and killing it? Mutt came into the kitchen, went over to his bowl and lapped up some water.

"I have to get that dog," she concluded, watching Mutt. "I have to."

The cold rain drenched Rose the moment she left the van. She couldn't find her raincoat and had to settle for her winter jacket, which was probably the best choice anyhow. A red raincoat would attract more attention than a black jacket.

She observed the house she planned on approaching and made sure no one was around. Then, taking the saw she'd brought and a small carrier, she moved cautiously toward the yard. Unlike the first time Rose entered Mrs. Green's yard, this time the gate was latched shut, but luckily it wasn't locked. She carefully opened the gate, stepped through and headed toward the rear of the backyard. A terrier mix greeted her with a friendly wag of her tail and, thankfully, no barking. The poor thing was soaked and obviously mistreated, yet still seemed trusting.

There was no chain holding this one. Only a thick rope. However, the dog's neck, under the rope, had an open laceration. Rose stifled a horrified gasped and tried to stay focused on why she was there.

Setting the carrier down next to a puddle, she pulled out a pocketknife.

She reached out for the end of the rope that was farthest from the dog, but the rope, being as wet as it was, kept slipping. Rose hacked away as fast as she could. Her motions agitated the terrier who began yelping and pulling on the rope.

"Come on," she muttered as the terrier kept barking and twisting the rope.

She pressed the knife harder into the rope until it finally gave way. As soon as she freed the animal, she put away the knife and took hold of the dog. Opening the carrier, she ushered it inside and closed the door behind it.

Securing the gate to the yard as she left, Rose looked around cautiously before taking the carrier and hurrying out to the street. She didn't want to run into Mrs. Green coming home early from her evening out.

As the rain dripped from her nose, down her neck and back, chilling her until her skin was a mass of goose bumps, she wondered what she was going to do with the terrier. She couldn't take another dog in.

She opened the side of her van and bent down to carefully place the carrier on the floor. "I'll take care of you inside the van," she assured the dog.

"I'm sure you will."

Rose shot up at the unexpected voice and hit her head on the door frame. She winced from the pain. "Ow!"

"A good knock on the head is exactly what you need. And I thought I'd seen it all."

Shocked as she recognized the voice, Rose rubbed her head and turned to Bob. Rain beaded the ends of his hair and his wet skin shone in the lone street lamp. He looked like a figure of melting ice standing before her. A very angry figure of melting ice. "When did you decide to spy on me?" she lashed out. "I don't recall you being a detective."

"I was coming home to see you as your van was pulling out of the driveway. I decided to follow you."

"This dog needed my help. Now please leave me alone. I

have to take care of it." She yanked the side door of the van quickly and closed it. She knew she shouldn't be so snippy with him, but the thought that he had followed her made her furious.

She moved past him so she could get into the car, but he grabbed her arm and pulled her close to his soaked body.

"There are better ways of saving dogs, Rose. What you're doing is against the law."

Rose tried to pull away, but he wouldn't let her move. "Let me go."

"Just stay put. I'm talking to you. I don't like you being a dog burglar."

"I'm not a dog burglar, Bob."

His grip tightened. "Then what are you?"

She looked up at him. His face was so angry. Oh God, he looked like he hated her.

"There's no nice way of putting it," he said. "You're a dog burglar. You're stealing someone else's dog and if you were anyone else, I'd be calling the police right now."

"Bob, you don't understand. This dog would have died in this woman's hands. Just like Mutt would have."

"Mutt? You mean to tell me you're stealing from the same person?"

"I'm not stealing anything from her." Rose struggled to free herself from Bob's grasp. "Don't you get it? These dogs are nothing but prisoners and there isn't a damn thing they can do for themselves. If I don't help them, they're as good as dead."

"Maybe you should have been a lawyer so you could have changed the laws."

"No. I should have been a cop," she said, still trying to break free. "So I could bust people committing crimes against defenseless animals."

"You can't bust them without a law on your side and the law only recognizes injury to a person, not an animal."

"Don't you think I know that?"

"If you want something done about it, head to the legislature."

"And in the time it takes to 'head to the legislature,'

these dogs will die. And I won't let that happen. I won't let them die the way Hardwin did. Now let me go, will you?"

"I'm not done talking to you."

"Well, I'm done talking to you! Now, let go or I'll kick you where it hurts!"

"If you promise not to steal another dog, I'll forget about all this."

"I don't want you to forget about all this! This means a lot to me. Don't you understand? Don't you see what I'm doing is important?"

"You knew from the beginning stealing a dog was wrong or you would have told me what you were doing."

Rose, shaking from the cold that was taking over her wet body, tried to speak. "If I told you, you would have gotten in the way and I can't bear to lose another dog! I won't lose another dog the way I lost Hardwin or the one that was choked to death! Now let go of me. I don't need you here!"

Bob's clenched jaw shifted. He pushed her away, sending her back against the van. Rose caught herself against the slippery metal of the car, trying not to fall.

"I don't need you either, Rose," he cried. "You hear that? I don't need you either! But think about this: What's in it for you? What are you getting out of all this?"

"This isn't for me!" she shouted back, pushing herself away from the car. "It's for these dogs!"

"Oh, is it? Is it?"

"Of course it is!"

"I think you're doing all this because it makes you feel good inside to know there are creatures on this planet that have it worse than you. You're lonely, aren't you? So lonely you want to grab onto anything that comes your way. And it doesn't matter what it is. A dog, a cat, me. You're using all of us. But, unlike a dog or a cat, I'm through being used."

Even if Bob had punched her, it wouldn't have hurt as much as what he said. Though he seemed to sense how deeply he wounded her, he didn't relent.

"That's right, Rose. The truth hurts. And now that you know it, it's all yours. The van, the dogs, everything. I don't want to see you ever again. You understand? My life's become hell."

He left her standing on the sidewalk and headed toward his car which was parked across the street. Rose slowly got into the van and sat behind the wheel, wiping the rain from her face. She turned the ignition and a whimper reminded her someone was waiting in the back. That whimper was exactly how she felt—desperate. She quietly wept. What now?

‍🐾 🐾 Chapter 18

Doggy Pickup

Rose lay on the couch watching Wiggles, Mutt, Valentine and Lucy exchange playful nips. Ever since Bob had left her for good that rainy night, she felt terribly lonely—even with the dogs around, even with her girls stopping in as often as they could. She looked at the phone beside the couch and wondered whether she should try calling him. She closed her eyes. If only she could will him to call her.

Suddenly, the phone rang. Her eyes flew open. Maybe it was him. She jumped up and grabbed for it.

"Hello?"

"Rose? Rose Block?"

"Yes?" she slowly replied to the clipped, English-sounding female voice on the phone.

"My name's Elizabeth Corey. I work as an investigator for the Humane Society."

Rose's heart jumped. "Yes?"

"I understand you filed two claims, the last one against a woman about a dog named Mutt, I believe. Do you remember the last claim you made?"

Rose sat back down on the couch and swallowed the lump in her throat. "Yes," she weakly replied.

"According to Mrs. Green, Mutt disappeared the day after you made the claim. Do you know anything about it?"

Rose closed her eyes. She knew she had to stay calm. She had to stay focused. Otherwise, they would end up taking Mutt away and she wasn't about to let them. Not after what she went through to save him. "Yes. Yes, I do."

"And?"

There was only one way to answer. Truthfully, with reservations. "I took him."

"You...took him. You mean you—"

"Yes, Ms. Corey. I got him out of Mrs. Green's yard."

"And what, may I ask, did you do with the dog?"

Rose hesitated, then said, "I took the dog to a no-kill shelter. He was adopted a few days after I brought him there. Luckily for the dog." Oh God, for someone who had never believed in lying it was getting to be a habit.

"So let me get this straight. You called us wanting to investigate Mrs. Green, only to take matters into your own hands?"

"Yes."

"Why?"

"Because the first time I reported a case of an abused dog to your organization, you did nothing and the dog was choked to death by its owner."

"I believe we did investigate that complaint. According to Mr. Woodson, the man you said was the owner, he never owned a dog."

Rose couldn't help the emotion in her voice. "You're joking! Did you even go into that man's backyard? There was a chain with a steel choke collar at the end of it that I wouldn't put around any animal, let alone an abused and starving dog that could hardly stand."

"There was no evidence of there ever being a dog on the premises. And if there isn't any evidence, we can't prove any abuse took place."

Rose sat down in the kitchen chair. "Did you go into the backyard?"

"He told me to check for myself and I did."

"And there was nothing?"

"Nothing."

Rose grimly shook her head. "I guess that shouldn't surprise me. Anyone who would do that to an animal would hide the evidence."

"Mrs. Block, I don't think you understand the seriousness of the situation. Setting aside the report on Mr. Woodson, let's get back to the one you recently made about Mrs. Green's dog."

"Of course," Rose bitterly replied. "Why would we want to dwell on a dog that was choked to death by its owner, who then hid all the evidence? Did I tell you I witnessed Woodson choking his dog to death?"

"I'm sorry you had to witness that. I'm sure it was horrible, but nevertheless you're not supposed to take matters into your own hands, Mrs. Block," the woman went on. "Stealing dogs is against the law."

"But killing them isn't?"

"I don't think you understand the consequences of your actions."

"I'm quite capable of understanding, Ms. Corey. What I did was save the dog that Mrs. Green was abusing. If I waited for you people to pick him up, he would have been dead, just like the other dog I called about. I've tried doing things the right way but I've gotten nowhere. Report me if you have to. Mutt's happy and that's all that matters."

There was a heavy sigh and the woman's tone of voice softened for a moment. "Even though a report should be filed against you, I have sympathy for what you think you witnessed, so let's just say I have too many other cases to deal with and filing a report against you would only put me further behind. But we can't support your actions. We are a legitimate agency that receives funding from a variety of sources that wouldn't look kindly upon our association with a dog thief."

Rose felt her cheeks beginning to flare along with her rising anger. "Oh, so I'm a dog thief? You don't consider what I did was a good thing?"

"I understand you did what you felt was right, but I don't have any proof that this woman or man abused animals as you said. I can't assume you're telling the truth and they're not. That's not exactly fair," the woman replied. "I'm in the business of helping dogs, but from my experience, you don't help dogs by stealing them from their owners based solely on the complaints of one individual. For all I know, you could be holding a grudge against Mrs. Green and Mr. Woodson and making up the complaint."

"That is absolutely untrue," Rose protested.

The woman interrupted. "Please, don't get me wrong. I'm sure you're a caring person looking out for the welfare of animals, but look at this from my perspective. I have one person making complaints, no other witnesses, no evidence and denials from the subjects of the complaints. I can't assume someone is guilty until proven innocent. Unfortunately, in such a case, my hands are tied. And, frankly, until we can totally understand the situation and be sure you're not breaking the law, we'll have to list you and not offer you any more aid, take any more complaints from you or assist you in any way."

"Do what you have to, but in the end, if organizations like yours can't help, then I believe something else is needed."

The woman bristled. "We have a fine organization. Everyone here works hard and puts in a lot of time and effort to help animals."

"I know you try, but somehow, a lot of animals are slipping through the cracks and dying."

"Look, Mrs. Block, I'm calling you on my time. I wasn't going to deal with this until Monday, but I wanted to talk to you before then. I wanted to hear your side of the story before jumping to any conclusions. I still think you know what you did is wrong."

"If you think what I did is wrong, perhaps you should consider what your organization doesn't do right!" Rose cried. "Waiting weeks to investigate neglected, abused and dying animals is wrong!" She angrily clicked the phone's OFF button.

She hated the idea that an organization that should be helping abused animals blacklisted the people who were trying to save them.

Ring.

Ring.

Rose stared at the cordless phone in her hand. *It had better not be that Elizabeth Corey calling back*, she thought.

"Yes, hello?"

"Is this Doggy Pickup?"

She smiled despite everything. "Royce. That's the nicest thing I've been called today."

"Well," he laughed, "you must be having problems. I hate to trouble you more, but you don't know the half of it. You remember that guy who was beating his dog? You know, the first time we met?"

"Yes. I just found out he has a name. Mr. Woodson."

"Mr. Woodson, huh? Well, I thought you should know this guy got himself another dog."

Rose felt her heart pound. The bastard got another dog? After telling the Humane Society he never owned one, let alone killed one?

"So, what are ya gonna do?"

She sighed. "Royce, I just got a call from the Humane Society and the woman told me they researched the complaints I filed against Mr. Woodson and Mrs. Green. Green is bad enough, but Woodson is violent. I don't think it's safe for me to go anywhere near him or his property."

"Yeah, but I've been watching his house. He went out earlier, but before he left, I heard him say to one of the neighbors he won't be back till tomorrow."

"You're sure?"

"Yeah. He asked the neighbor to keep an eye on his house for him. You could go there and take his dog."

Rose shook her head. "I don't know if that's such a good idea, Royce. That guy's crazy. What if the neighbor sees me and calls him or calls the police? You know, he choked to death the last dog I tried to get from him to death."

He let out a low whistle. "That S.O.B.! Not that it should surprise me, the way he's been kicking this new dog in the head. Man, I thought he killed her this afternoon, but she was just out."

"You mean, he kicked it so hard the dog lost consciousness?"

"Yeah, but that ain't half as bad as what he did to her back leg."

"Her leg?" Rose felt queasy. She didn't want to know. She really didn't think she could handle any more today.

"He carved his initials into the dog's back leg in broad daylight. Right there in the front of his house."

She closed her eyes in disbelief, as if she had just witnessed it. "He did this in full view of the entire neighborhood?"

"Sure did. Yesterday, in the front yard while I was sittin' on the curb on the other side of the street. One kid who was walking by just about went into fits when he saw it."

Rose could guess who the kid was. It probably was little Mike. The poor kid. She couldn't imagine witnessing something like that.

"You there?"

"Yes, Royce, I'm here," she quietly said. "What does the dog look like?"

"It's yellow and pretty small—a puppy, I guess—about half the size of the first dog he had. You can take it by yourself, no problem. Unless the dog's the biting sort." He coughed. "Man, it's cold out here. And it's snowin' like crazy. You'd think we were up in the North Pole."

"Just one more thing, Royce," she hurriedly added. "Where does he keep the dog? I assume it's outside."

Royce coughed again. "He's only had the dog a couple of days, but from what I saw, yeah, he chains the dog outside in the backyard."

"Thanks for calling, Royce. Wait out front for me so I can pay you."

"Nah, nah, not tonight. It's too damn cold. I'm headin' to the shelter."

"Alright. I'll get you next time, though."

"Sounds good. So, you're gonna get her tonight?"

"I'm on my way."

"You're one good lady."

"Thank you, Royce. It's nice to know someone thinks so."

After hanging up, Rose went into the kitchen and placed the cordless phone in its recharging stand on the kitchen counter. She took a deep breath.

The bastard! He actually carved his name into the dog's leg. She felt like he was taunting her. Daring her to come get the new dog. Well, she wasn't going to back down from this challenge.

She turned to look at the kitchen clock. It was nine at night. She didn't realize it was already that late. If she left within the next twenty minutes, she could get the dog and be back home by ten-thirty or so.

She peered out the kitchen window. It was early March and a late winter snow was heavily falling. The weather certainly wasn't going to make the drive there any easier, however it would ensure that few people would be out and about to witness anything.

Mutt pranced into the kitchen, breaking Rose from her reverie. He went over to his bowl, lapped up some water and sauntered back out. Valentine yawned and did her best to stretch out in front of the refrigerator. Wiggles barked somewhere from the living room and Lucy was no doubt sleeping on the bed. And the cats? The cats were probably hiding, as they seemed to do more and more lately. Though there wasn't much love lost between them and the dogs, peace thankfully reigned when everyone stayed out of each other's way.

"I have to go out again," she said softly told them. "No one else will help you guys."

The snow was blinding and the wind freezing. Rose felt the bitter cold bite right through her layers of clothing the moment she stepped out of the van.

She had worn her white winter jacket to hide her better in the brightness of the whirling snow. She observed the house, the same house that still gave her chills just thinking about the dog that had been choked to death on the premises. She waited to make sure no one was around.

The lights were off, just as Royce had told her they would be, and from what she could make out, no one was peering from the any windows. She only hoped this Woodson guy hadn't changed his mind and returned home early, especially with the weather being so bad.

She gripped the black bag she had stuffed with tools she thought she might need, then slogged toward the backyard, the piling snow slowing her steps.

A small yellow Labrador retriever mix in a large handmade cage greeted her without any barking. The poor thing was lifting each leg in turn, trying to keep its feet out of the knee-high, freezing snow. The brightness of the snow reflected everything, including dark red spots dripping from the dog's paw. It was blood from the carved leg.

Except for a padlock on the cage, there was no other barrier to keep her getting the dog free from the cage. However, Rose would also have to cut off a thick rope around the dog's neck before taking the animal.

Although she hadn't expected a wire cage, she knew it would be easy enough to open. She had brought wire cutters as well as a saw. She figured the better the tools she had, the quicker she could get things done.

She dropped the black bag, took off her gloves and pulled out the wire cutters. Her fingers were already growing numb in the wind and snow that whirled around her. Inspecting the crude, rusted cage embedded in the snow, she decided to cut the right side. She had to make an opening wide enough so she could crawl inside and cut the rope from around the dog's neck.

"Here we go," she said aloud.

She gripped the icy metal and, although her fingers immediately stuck to it and began burning, she held on tight, keeping it in place. Cut after hard cut, she worked her way down the side of the cage, tugging her fingers away from the metal every now and then to keep going.

That Woodson bastard probably didn't think she would

come out in this sort of weather just to rescue a dog. Maybe taking this dog would stop him from getting another one.

Once there was enough wire cut, Rose peeled the section down and began crawling into the cage. Her fingers had grown numb and the blood-spotted snow her bare hands sunk into actually felt warmer than the metal she had been working on.

Once inside the cage, she could make out that the Labrador was a she. Even in the few days that the man had her, the dog had suffered far too much.

Rose stuffed the wire cutters into her coat pocket and withdrew her husband's favorite pocketknife. She momentarily wondered what Bob would think if he knew she was using his knife for this.

The dog suddenly jerked far off to the side, yelping, barking and hitting the side of the cage.

It took Rose a few moments to realize that it was the knife she was holding that scared the dog. The man had probably carved its leg with a similar knife. Tears sprung to her eyes, her heart aching for all the pain the animal had been through.

She reached out to the farthest part of the rope. "Darn, it's frozen." It was almost too hard to cut through.

"Come on," she muttered, as the dog continued to bark and twist the rope away.

She pressed the knife harder into the rope and sliced it using the weight of her body. Finally it gave way. She held on to the rope, using it as a leash, and put the knife back into her pocket. Crawling backwards out of the cage, she coaxed the dog out.

Taking one last look around, she shoved her hands back into her gloves and picked up the bag. She bent over to try to pick the dog up, but it let out a low growl.

"Alright, then I'll walk you real slow," she said soothingly.

Slowly, Rose led the dog out, making sure she was careful of the injured leg. The dog began moving forward slowly. As a blast of wind and snow hit Rose's face and body, she shivered, chilled to the bone. Thank God they were getting out of this weather.

When she reached her van, she opened the side door so the dog could get inside. It didn't take much prodding, since the car was still warm and, like her, the puppy wanted to get out of the foul weather. One leg at a time and a push to the Labrador's rear and the dog was inside, moving into the farthest corner in the back. Rose leaned in and arranged an open can of dog food on one of the seats so the dog could reach it. Then she hurriedly shut the door and looked around once more. She examined the neighboring houses for signs of someone checking on Mr. Woodson's house but everything was still and quiet. She quickly went around to the other side of the van and climbed in.

Sliding the key into the ignition, Rose turned and looked at the dog snuggling in the blankets in the backseat and breathed a sigh of relief. Then, letting the handbrake up and pressing the gas pedal down hard, she sped away into the swirling snow.

❖ ❖ Chapter 19

A Hurt Dog, a Future Pet

That Saturday, when the casts were due to come off Valentine's hind legs, Rose eagerly awaited the dog's first steps. It was a miracle that Valentine would no longer have to lie in front of the refrigerator on her side, only pulling up and dragging herself around to eat.

Now she watched Valentine stand on all four legs in the middle of the clinic examination room, staring at Rose as if something profoundly glorious had happened. Despite the dog's awareness that she was now free from the shackles of the casts she had been bound to these past few weeks, she didn't dare move. Valentine just stood there, her legs stiff and wobbly, uncertain what she should do.

"Come on, Valentine," she whispered to her. "Come over here, sweetie."

But Valentine didn't budge.

"It'll take some time for her to adjust to walking," the vet said, bending over Valentine to examine her legs one last time. "But she'll be fine. She'll be just fine. In no time, she'll be running in circles."

Running in circles, but where? Rose sadly thought. She had promised Bob that Valentine would go to a shelter as soon as her legs were healed. That day was now, as much as she hated to face it.

She had grown attached to Valentine, because she was always in the kitchen, beating her tail against the tile floor whenever Rose walked by. And whenever she or Bob wanted something out of the refrigerator, Valentine let out a playful bark, knowing she would be giving up for a moment her favorite space in the world.

"Make sure she doesn't do too much walking at once," the vet cautioned, interrupting Rose's thoughts.

Rose blankly nodded. She wondered whether she could talk Bob into keeping Valentine. *Bob.* Funny how she was still concerned about bringing dogs home and how Bob would react when in reality, she didn't have to worry about that. Bob was no longer there. She felt a pang of loneliness and tried to erase those thoughts by focusing on Valentine.

"Would you like to come home with me?" she finally asked.

Valentine answered with a happy bark.

"Well, it's settled then."

On the way home, Rose decided to drive through Dalton City.

"Do you think I'm crazy?" she asked Valentine, glancing toward the back seat.

Valentine lifted her head in response but gave no other answer.

"I guess everyone's crazy to a certain extent. We all just have our individual forms of insanity," she murmured, turning the wheel to head down little Mike's snow-covered street. She wondered how he was and if he liked the book she had given him for his birthday.

Suddenly, she saw him. Mike was sitting at the bottom of his shoveled front steps, his head bent over something. He looked busy, if not fascinated, with whatever he was doing.

"Wait here in the car while I go talk to him," Rose said to Valentine, parking the car.

Valentine shifted in the backseat and yawned.

"I'll take that as a yes and hurry up."

Only when Rose slammed the door to her van did Mike look up. A huge grin came over his face when he saw her.

"Thanks, Rose! I love it," he exclaimed, hugging something to his chest.

"I'm glad." She smiled, moving closer.

He sprang up on his booted feet and proudly held up the present she'd bought him—an encyclopedia all about dogs.

"I've been studying this. Now I'll be able to tell you what sort of dogs I find," he excitedly said. "I didn't even know there were this many dog breeds in the world. Curly-haired, shorthaired, straighthaired, longhaired. Did you know that the one gray dog I called you about that was chained to the car is actually not gray but blue?"

"Blue?"

"Yeah. There are all different types of colors and one color we thought was gray is actually a kinda blue."

"Really?" she said, fascinated by the amount of knowledge he had already absorbed.

"Yeah. Hey, it's a good thing you're here." He stood up, unzipped the front of his winter jacket and shoved the book inside. "I was gonna call you, but Grandma wouldn't let me. She says I bother you too much."

Rose smiled. "You can bother me any time, Mike."

"Come on. I want to show you something." He hurried past her and started heading down the block.

"Mike, I can't go right now," she called, walking after him. "I have to take Valentine home. She had the casts taken off her legs today."

He paused and looked sad. "This one dog got into a fight with a pack. I'm not sure but he might have an infection from the bites and I think maybe you should look at him. I think he's got some shepherd and pit bull in him, but you don't have to be afraid."

Rose couldn't believe the volume of information he had turned into. "How do you know what mix he is?"

"The ears, the face, you know, and the way he stands. He looks like a shepherd and a pit put together, just like in the picture in here." He tapped on the book through his jacket.

"Mike, I just can't believe how much you've already learned."

"I told you I've been studying the different types of dogs that are around here. There sure are a lot of them."

"So what about this dog you want me to see?" she asked, crunching toward him through the snow.

"I just want you to check up on him and see if he'll be okay. He belongs to some people on the next street and I don't think they've even looked at him since the fight."

Rose glanced toward the van and seeing no movement from within, figured Valentine was sleeping. "Maybe we should get a leash, just in case."

To her surprise, Mike pulled one out of his pocket. "I have one already. Are you coming?"

"Where'd you get that?" she asked pointing at the gray leash.

"Grandma got it for me after I begged her. Now I can go get the dogs on the street, then call you so you can pick them up."

Pausing just a few steps away from him, Rose stared down at him, his face beaming at what he held in his small, tight fist. "Mike, I don't want you doing anything your grandmother wouldn't approve of," she finally said.

He was quiet for a moment, then stuffed the leash back into his pocket and shrugged. "You taught me that you gotta do what you gotta do for these dogs. They don't have anyone but us."

She grinned. As if everything he had done for her, as if his apparent fascination and love for dogs wasn't enough to melt her heart, his words expressed exactly what she felt. "Mike, you are one great kid, you know that?"

"So you and Grandma say. Come on. You gotta see this dog."

As they trudged through the snowdrifts no one had bothered to shovel in the past few days, the cold wind picked up.

"The dog's outside lying in the snow," Mike said, crossing someone's front yard to turn the corner quicker. "He's been out there all week. Just two days ago, I saw he was bit up pretty bad. His legs, his ears, his neck. It doesn't look good."

"And you didn't call me?" she asked, trying to keep up with him.

"Grandma wouldn't let me call. She really gets all upset with me for lying to her, which is why I decided to ask her for a leash for my birthday. I figured you'd be around sooner or later. You're never gone for more than a day or two." He paused, then pointed to a house across the street. "There. You see him?"

At the bottom of the unshoveled walkway of one of the dilapidated brick houses Rose could make out a furry, chocolate colored head sticking out of the snow. "It looks as if the dog's body is completely buried," she said worriedly.

"After he got into the fight, he went and dug a hole to crawl into," he commented.

"Poor thing. The snow's probably not only soothing his wounds but actually keeping him warm." She sighed. She wasn't expecting to rescue a dog today.

"He's not tied," Mike tempted her, taking out the leash. "And he knows me, 'cause I've been throwing him food. You want me to go get him? He's really friendly."

"Let's get a good look at him first. Do you know his name?"

"Nope. I never heard him called anything."

"Okay. Come on."

Together, they approached, slow and steady. The dog raised its head as Mike and Rose drew closer, as if he was waiting to see what they would do.

Three steps nearer and he scooted out of the snow hole and limped up the stairs. Rose saw now that his front and hind legs appeared covered with sores. He settled into the far corner of the porch and watched them with eyes as they moved steadily closer. They took a few more steps and a growl and a bark escaped him.

"I thought you said he was friendly," Rose whispered to Mike.

"He is. But he don't know you."

Rose paused and stared at the chocolate-colored dog.

"He doesn't appear to be starving." No bones stuck out and although his fur looked unkempt and sores covered his ears, legs and neck, he looked otherwise healthy.

It was apparent that his owners took better care of him than most of the others dogs she'd rescued. She felt like she needed to give the owner of the dog a chance to explain. "Maybe they don't know the dog is hurt," she said.

Mike shrugged and adjusted the bulky front of his jacket that hid his encyclopedia. "Maybe."

She looked toward the windows of the house and noticed a dim light beyond the crookedly hung curtains. "Let's knock on the door and talk to them before we assume anything."

Mike stared at her as if she had either lost her mind or done something wrong. "What do you mean, knock on the door?" he asked incredulously. "I thought you'd want to take him out of there. He needs help."

"But look closely at him," Rose whispered, pointing to the dog who continued to watch them. "He looks healthy except for those bites. He has a collar that's been regularly adjusted and these people feed him. He's not thin."

"Yeah, so?"

Rose sighed. It was apparent that it didn't matter to Mike whether the dog was being fed or not. He only saw a dog covered with sores and bites lying out in the snow in sub-zero weather and no shelter in sight except for the one he had dug for himself in the snow.

"They should have taken him to the vet the second it happened," Mike angrily pointed out. "I mean, he's got cuts all over him. I looked at him real close yesterday morning and I saw that part of his ear got chewed off. He might even need surgery to fix it."

"You're sounding like a vet," Rose said, unable to withhold a smile. She certainly thought he'd make one heck of a veterinarian. Not only because of his interest in animals, but because of his compassion for them.

"Well?" he prompted.

"Maybe they can't afford a vet," she ventured. "I mean, sometimes I think I can't even afford these vets. They're really expensive, and, depending on what's wrong with the dog, it can cost hundreds, if not over a thousand dollars for medication, surgery, food, you name it. Now you wait here, okay? I'll be right back."

"What are you gonna do?"

"Just stay here."

She walked up the rest of the stairs and paused at the paint-peeling door behind a wire screen that hung crookedly on its hinges.

"I'm just making a visit," she murmured to herself. She carefully opened the screen door, afraid it might fall off, and knocked.

A few minutes later, a young woman in her mid-twenties came to the door, her two ponytails coming out of their hastily-applied rubber bands. "Yeah?" she asked, staring at Rose.

"Hi. My name is Rose. I help dogs in the area."

"Yeah, I know. I've heard of you," she quickly replied. "So what do you want?"

"I just wanted to know if that's your dog?" Rose pointed toward the end of the porch.

The woman didn't even look. "Yeah, why?"

"Did you know he got attacked by another dog? He looks like he's in pretty bad shape. I thought you should know."

The woman was quiet for a moment, then peered out past the screen door and looked toward the dog. "Hey, Baby. Baby, come here," she said in a low, sweet voice.

The dog's tail started wagging for the first time since Rose and Mike approached. He struggled to stand only to let out a whimper as he feebly limped toward them.

"Oh, God, Baby, what'd you do?" The woman, who only had a pair of slippers on to protect her feet, stepped around Rose and squatted down in the snow. Reaching out, she took the dog by the collar and tugged him to her. "Damn it, you're bleeding," she whispered, checking his ears, then his neck. "When did all this happen?"

"According to my little friend, Mike, here," Rose offered, glancing toward him, "it was about two days ago. Did you see it happen, Mike?"

"Not the whole thing. But I saw the end of it. He and this other really big dog were making so much noise, I went out to see what was going on. By the time I got there, the other dog was gone and this dog was laying in the snow and he didn't move for a long time. Even when I called to him and came up to him. I thought he was dead, but I guess he was just in shock." He adjusted the front of his jacket. "I knocked on the door of your house, but no one was home so I just stayed with him a little while until I knew for sure he was going to be okay. I watched him get up and nose his way into the snow, probably to keep himself warm. He was whimpering the whole time, like he was in a lot of pain and I knew he ought to see a vet."

The woman continued observing the open cuts on the dog, her face scrunching up in what could only be anguish for the animal. "Damn it, Baby," she scolded. "You know you're not supposed to go past the house. How did you get involved in fighting another dog?"

"He shouldn't be outside the house," Rose insisted. "It's freezing. Aren't you worried about him getting frostbite?"

"He doesn't like being in the house too long. He gets stir crazy and starts ripping things apart. He scratches on the door till I let him out."

"So you leave him outside for days on end?" Rose sharply commented.

The woman glared at her, then stood up. "I treat my dog good, do you understand? I don't hit him, I don't chain him, I feed him whatever we can afford to and he gets plenty of hugs."

"He shouldn't be out in this weather."

"Yeah, well, you tell the dog that," the woman snapped. "He prefers being outside."

"If you're going to leave him outside, he should at least have some kind of doghouse. It's the law, you know. Dogs have to have shelter if they're left outside."

"Law or no law, those doghouses are too expensive," she responded, clearly agitated. "You think I like leaving him outside like this? He wants to go outside and claws the door 'til it drives me crazy. What do you want me to do?"

"I understand some dogs are like that," Rose softly offered, trying not to offend the woman. "What about a vet? You have to take him to the vet. Just look at him. He needs help."

The woman sighed and shook her head. "I can't afford a vet, okay? I got some rubbing alcohol in the house. Won't that work?"

Although Rose felt she was beginning to understand that this woman took care of her dog as best as she knew how, Rose was still very concerned. Judging by the several layers of grungy T-shirts the woman was wearing, she couldn't even afford to buy warm winter clothing for herself, let alone take a dog to a veterinary clinic.

"Your dog needs more than rubbing alcohol," Rose finally said in an understanding tone. "He might need stitches and, depending on the damage done, even surgery."

"So what do you want me to do?" the woman demanded, waving a hand at Rose. "I ain't no doctor and, like I said, I can't afford one."

Rose didn't have to think about the words that spilled forth from her mouth. "Let me pay for whatever care he needs."

The young woman stared at Rose as if she didn't understand what Rose had said. "Say again?"

Rose smiled. "Let me take him to the veterinarian. I'll pay the cost of treatment and then I'll bring him back to you good as new. But only if you promise to make him some sort of doghouse. We have a workshop at home and I can bring you some wood."

The woman crossed her arms and rubbed them as if suddenly affected by the bitterness of the cold. "You're kidding me, right? I mean, why would you wanna do something like that?"

"Because the dog needs help," Rose explained. "And I think you know that. He needs expert medical attention and the sooner the better."

The woman gave Rose a last lingering look, then walked past her, opening the screen door to her house. She whistled, as she opened it wider. "Come on, Baby. Let's go inside. It's cold out."

"Is that his name, Baby?" Rose watched the dog limp as fast as he could past her.

"Yeah." She ushered the dog inside, then leaned in toward her and whispered, "My husband's in the house right now and I know for a fact he don't like taking charity. He's the proud sort, you know. But how about you come back tomorrow? Around eight? He works in the early morning."

Rose smiled at the woman and nodded. "I'll be here."

"And what was your name again? Rose?"

"Yes, Rose."

"My name's Donna."

"Well, it's nice to you meet you, Donna," Rose said, nodding. "And I'm glad you aren't offended by my offer. I just want to help. I'll bring over the wood tomorrow morning so you and your husband can get right on it."

"Thanks. You have a good day now and I'll see you tomorrow at eight." The woman smiled and held up a quick hand before shutting the door.

"So she's going to let you take it to the vet?" Mike asked from behind Rose.

She nodded, turning. "Yes. Tomorrow."

"Why tomorrow?" he insisted. "He's in really bad shape."

"I know that, Mike. I know that." Rose took the boy by the hand and directed him down the snowy steps of the porch. "But he'll be okay for one more day as long as he's inside."

"Why didn't she let you take him now?" he whined in concern. "He's gotta see the vet right away."

Rose patted him on the back and tried to patiently explain. "Sometimes, Mike, the owners aren't cruel. They just don't know how to care for a pet," she said. "And this is one of those times. These people are proud and don't have a lot of money, but that doesn't mean they don't have the right to have a dog. I'm not saying they're doing a great job, because I don't like the idea of a dog being kept outside in cold weather like this even if he hadn't been wounded, but at least their hearts are in the right place. Do you understand what I'm saying?"

Mike took a deep breath and let it out. "I guess I understand."

"Good."

"So the dog's name is Baby?"

"Yep."

"Did you see the pit bull in him, like I told you?"

Rose glanced down at him and smiled. "I gave him a good look over and I don't see the pit in him. He looks more shepherd than anything, with maybe a bit of chow in him. Definitely more chow than pit."

Mike shook his head. "Nah ah. He's definitely got pit bull in him. Didn't you see the way he stands? His jaw? His muscles? There's definitely pit in him." He pulled away from her and put his hand under his jacket, taking out his book.

He quickly thumbed through it. When he stopped, he brought the book close to his face and read, " 'Well put together, pit bull terriers are muscular with ears set high. The tail is short in comparison to size, tapering to a fine visible point. Jaw is well defined with lips close together and no looseness.'" He looked up at her, his large eyes dancing with the pleasure of knowledge. "That describes him, doesn't it?"

"Many dogs fit that description, Mike."

"The vet would know for sure, right?"

"Yes."

He slapped his book shut and shoved it under his jacket again. "So can I go with you tomorrow? I can help you bring Baby there."

Rose tilted her head and playfully eyed him. "I guess so. Tomorrow's Saturday and let me guess. You want to go to the vet so you can prove me wrong about the sort of mix Baby is? Is that it?"

Mike let out a giggly laugh as he hurried onward, toward his house. "Yeah," he called out. "So I can prove you wrong!"

"I think I know more about dogs than you do," she teasingly called after him. "Who started this whole thing anyway?"

"We're going to have to clip the hair from all the bitten areas, clean him up and see where we go from there," the veterinarian explained as he examined Baby. "At the bare minimum, he's going to need antibiotics to fight infection. Hopefully, these are nothing more than punctures, so that he won't need any sutures."

Rose nodded. "Could you give him a bath first? I don't think he's had a bath in a while."

Dr. Bild, the vet, shook his head. "Not today. We don't have time. We close in a couple hours."

"But don't you think that—"

"And besides," he went on, "we wouldn't want to bathe him with his sores being the way they are."

"I guess that makes sense." She looked over at Mike who was leaning on the counter in the far corner, looking curiously at some of the chrome instruments then back down at Baby who sat patiently trying to understand what was going on. "Is there any way you can keep Baby overnight for observation?" she finally asked.

"Well, seeing as it's Saturday, we're not going to be here for much longer. There's no way we could observe him over the weekend," Dr. Bild explained. "I mean, somebody comes in tomorrow twice to do feedings, but that's it."

"So you can't keep him?" she asked in concern.

"Of course we can, I think you've been here enough to know we take good care of the animals. And I doubt if he'd have any problems on his own until Monday, if you wanted us to keep him here on the weekend. But, just so you know, there's no one that's actually going to be here around the clock."

She nodded. "I understand."

"So what kind of dog do you think he is?" Mike asked, coming up to them.

Dr. Bild looked Baby over, then said, "Definitely shepherd and pit bull mix."

"Told ya!" Mike boastfully looked at Rose. "Just like it said in the book."

Rose swatted at him, making him laugh, before asking the vet, "So what makes you say pit bull?"

"The head and the front of the nose."

"Told ya!" Mike said again.

"Now, judging by the collar, he's not the usual type of stray you bring in, am I right?" the vet asked.

"Right. I'm bringing him in for a friend."

"Good, okay. Let's start by taking the collar off. It's too small anyway." The vet leaned over and carefully undid the buckle. As he slipped the collar off from around the dog's neck, Baby let out a growl, as if he had hurt him.

"It's okay, Baby," Rose whispered.

"You should really get him a new, larger collar," Dr. Bild said, holding up the one he had detached from around Baby's mane.

"I'll do that and bring it when I pick him up," Rose nodded.

"Can I have that, if you're gonna give him a new one?" Mike asked, coming up to him. "I collect dog collars."

"Sure. Here."

Mike took the collar and held it as if he had won something of great value.

"Since when did you start collecting collars?" Rose asked.

"Since I first started helping you. I got all sorts now."

"All right, then, we'll take good care of him," the vet said, interrupting their conversation. "You can come back for him sometime next week. We'll call you."

"Thank you." Rose leaned over and looked Baby in the eyes. As much as she wanted to pet him, she knew he wouldn't take kindly to her hands near his cuts. "You be a good boy," she told him.

Baby looked up at the doctor, seemingly content.

Rose sighed and signaled for Mike to follow her out.

• • • •

When Rose and Mike drove up to Donna's house to give her the news on Baby and tell Donna that she could expect her dog home sometime next week, Rose was surprised to find the woman outside in the snow, the pieces of wood Rose had earlier dropped off all around her.

Dressed in a thin sweatshirt with a hammer in her hand, Donna was working hard putting together the pieces of wood, which were beginning to resemble a lopsided little house with half a roof. Rose watched as she dropped the hammer, picked up a saw and began cutting another piece of wood that lay at her feet half-hidden in the snow.

Seeing Donna working so hard and doing her best with whatever fortitude and knowledge she had trying to build a doghouse touched Rose. She knew her instincts about the woman were right. Donna definitely deserved Baby.

"You need some help?" Rose called out, getting out of the van and heading toward Donna.

Donna looked up, the saw halfway through the piece of wood on which she was working and shook her head. "I'm okay. At least, I think I am. All I have left to do is to nail the roof on."

"Let me hold it for you."

"Good. I'll be able to finish cutting this last piece." Donna sawed through the wood. "There."

"I can't believe you did all this in just three hours," Rose commented, taking the wood from Donna and placing it on the side of the open slant.

"I figured my husband wasn't going to do it and Baby deserves a house, seeing he's outside so much."

"Baby will love you all the more," Rose murmured, still holding the side of the roof in place.

"I know he will." Donna steadied a nail, then hit the hammer repeatedly against it. "So what did the vet say? Are they going to be able to fix him up?"

"Yes, Baby will be fine. They're keeping him until next week."

"The doctor gave me his collar," Mike announced, coming up to them. "Rose is going to get Baby a new one."

Donna paused and stared at the collar Mike held up. "Why did he need a new collar? That one's just fine."

Mike continued to dangle the collar before him. "It's too small."

"He's had it since he was a puppy. It's the only thing my husband ever got him."

Mike's arm fell, and he suddenly looked melancholy, her words clearly affecting him. "Did you want the collar? Rose is getting Baby a new one, but you can still keep this."

Donna shook her head. "That's okay. Joe will understand."

"So I can keep it?"

She smiled. "Yeah."

"Great, thanks! I'll be right back to help. I'm gonna go run this over to my house."

Rose and Donna watched Mike skid across the street, fall over in a pile of snow, scramble up and disappear around the corner.

"He's a really good kid," Donna said. "You don't come across many of those anymore."

"He's an incredible kid." Rose smiled warmly at her. "And when he grows up, he's going to make an incredible veterinarian. I just know it."

Billy/Butch

From where Rose sat in the van, she could see that beneath its facade of burnt out and abandoned structures, littered lots and dilapidated houses was the truth that the rest of the world, comfortable in its prosperity, did not see. The truth that life for most dogs and human beings in neighborhoods such as this one was about survival; survival against hunger, survival against weather and survival against others.

She watched as a beautifully colored dog whose tones of red, brown and black showed it to be a chow mix with a bit of collie and shepherd, peacefully lay in the front yard of one of the houses. He was horribly thin, as were many of the strays in the neighborhood, only he was no stray. There was a collar around his neck claiming ownership and the property he was on made it clear where he belonged.

Suddenly, two children ran out through the front door, yelling and hooting, a baseball bat, ball and mitt in hand. Though there was still snow on the ground, it was an unseasonably mild day. After months of frigid temperatures, even one day at fifty degrees seemed to spark spring fever in the young boys. The dog looked up from where it lay, its ears perked and its tail still, barely acknowledging them.

The kids headed into the street and started playing, ignoring the animal on the lawn. The dog watched the ball with fascination. Back and forth, back and forth, like a child seeing the circus for the first time.

As the bat connected with the ball the next time, the smaller boy hit it in the direction of the dog. One of the kids started yelling something.

Rose rolled down her window to hear the words being said.

"Hey Butch! Get the ball. Bring the ball here!"

Butch looked at the ball that had rolled within two feet of him and then laid down his head, ignoring the request.

"Butch!" one of the boys shouted. "I know you heard me! Get the ball!"

The dog continued to lay there, unmoving.

"You know he never gets the ball," the taller boy in the red shirt said disgustedly. "He's stupid."

"Dogs are anything but stupid," Rose whispered to herself.

"I said get the ball, Butch!" the boy harshly ordered. "Get it!"

Butch lifted his head, sensing his owner's urgency, got up and slowly walked over to the ball. He bent his head and scooped it up. Then he stood there, looking at them.

"Come here! NOW!"

The beautifully colored dog continued to stare at them, head somewhat lowered, but otherwise did not obey the command.

The taller boy crossed over to Butch, baseball bat in hand. Rose tensed, afraid of what the boy might be planning to do. He was just a child and children never sought to bring harm to others. Unless, of course, they were taught to do so.

Pausing before the dog, the boy stretched out his hand. "Give it to me, Butch. I said, give it to me!"

The dog inched back.

The kid with the red shirt bent down and tried snatching the ball away from the dog. Suddenly, the dog growled and bared his teeth. The boy jumped back, ran around the dog, up the front porch steps and into the house.

Butch looked back toward the house and something he saw made him drop the ball. He stood there, waiting.

Within moments, the front door banged open and the boy with the red shirt was followed out by a man. Presumably, the man was the boy's father. Rose looked closer. The boy no longer had the baseball bat in his hand. The father now held the bat.

"I'll teach you to try to bite my kid!" the man angrily cried. He ran toward the dog and swung the bat at the dog's head. The crack resounded in Rose's ears. A yelp escaped the dog as it dashed backwards, its head lowered to the ground in submission.

Rose put her hand to the car door, ready to interject, but the man threw aside the bat, said something to his son and went back inside the house.

The boy looked toward the dog, picked up the ball, then his bat and went back out into the street. The dog, its head lowered, scooted toward the side of the house and lay down, watching the two boys and quietly whimpering in a pitiful manner.

Rose felt herself trembling. She took a deep breath trying to calm down. If the owner could take a baseball bat to the dog's head, who knew what else he could do to the animal? She was scared for Butch. Scared that the next time, he might not survive. And she knew she had to do something before another crack of the bat killed him.

Late that night, she returned to Dalton City. The only lights of the house that were on were toward the rear of the structure. She quietly got out of the van and made her approach. Because the dog wasn't tied, she knew it would be easy to take him. With a leash in one hand and a warm beef sandwich in the other, she crept toward the shadowy creature still lying in the snow. He hadn't moved since that afternoon.

She held out the beef sandwich and waved it about, hoping to send the scent in his direction. His head went up.

"Come here, Butch," she whispered, slowly waving it before the animal. "Come here."

Butch watched her from the shadows for a moment longer before dropping his head to the ground again, uninterested.

Rose knew he was interested in the beef sandwich but he was acting out the same part he had when those boys were playing baseball. It was curiosity in the form of aloofness. That was probably the only way he survived. Pretending he didn't care.

She was sure Butch wanted the sandwich, even if he didn't seem to. He was mostly fur and bones and who knew when the last time was that he had been fed by his so-called human family? Poor Butch was just like so many others she saw. Chained to the idea of being a family pet without any benefits. The only sort of physical touch it knew was related to beatings. And shelter? That consisted of hiding beneath parked cars, which was really no different than being beneath a bare tree during a winter storm.

Butch cared about his existence, all right. If he didn't, he would have given up and died long ago.

Rose inched closer, holding the beef sandwich out so he could sniff it as the sign of peace she offered. He didn't move, only continued watching her advance.

"How about we call you Billy instead of Butch?" she gently asked, coming as close as she could. "You're nothing like that family of yours."

She carefully unwrapped the sandwich from the thin wax paper that surrounded it, tucked the gravy-stained wrapper into her pocket and placed the sandwich within a foot of him, waiting for the dog to get it. She squatted, leash ready, waiting for his advance.

Butch played a mind game of will. Fifteen minutes later, the sandwich still lay where Rose had placed it, untouched and uneaten.

"Come on, Billy," she murmured, adjusting the leash.

"You don't want to live like this for the rest of your life. Let me help you."

For the first time since she approached him, he lifted his head. It was as if her words had touched him and he was seriously considering his position in life.

"Let me help you," she said again, knowing that even if he didn't understand what she was saying he could sense her caring.

The animal, still showing strong uncertainty, slowly rose and began inching closer and closer to the sandwich. However, he wasn't looking at the sandwich; he kept his eyes locked on her.

"Let me help you," she again whispered the words of assurance that seemed to draw him near.

He paused and after another moment, took the beef sandwich in his jaws and quickly chewed and swallowed a large piece of it as if he was afraid Rose might take the food away if he hesitated.

When he had practically devoured the whole sandwich and his head lowered for the last bite, Rose looped the leash around his neck and tightened it.

He let out a low growl and showed his teeth in response. It was the same sort of response that had scared the boy in the red shirt earlier in the day, but Rose wasn't about to back down.

"I'm going to help you, Billy," she assured him, making the leash tighter with a gentle yank.

Rose pulled, now asking the dog to follow her. He didn't resist, but he didn't come with a great amount of willingness, either.

"Come on, Billy. Let's go." She led him to the van and opened the door as quietly as she could, so as not to startle Billy or draw attention to herself.

"Go on in," she said, lifting the leash to guide him inside.

The animal hesitated, but finally jumped in. She smiled. He was safe. She drove right to Dr. Bild who raised his eyebrows as Rose walked into his office with Billy. "That's number three this week, Rose. Take it easy."

She smiled at him wearily. "I wish I could, but there's just too many that need me."

When Rose went to pick up Billy from the vet a week later, she was saddened to hear that he was heartworm positive. Not that it should have been a surprise. Many of the dogs she rescued were heartworm positive. Heartworm simply meant neglect. And although Dr. Bild had already started to treat the dog, it would be a matter of weeks before they knew if the animal was rid of the parasites.

She knew she couldn't take Billy home with her, if only for the fact that he had heartworm. The treatment would mean he should be temporarily isolated.

"There's something else," Dr. Bild said thoughtfully. "Billy has a tendency to be on the aggressive side," the vet pointed out to her. "He bit two of our assistants. It's from the abuse, I'm guessing, not to mention the chow in him. Chows have a tendency to get aggressive."

Rose grew worried. Biting was not a good sign. How was she ever going to adopt a biting dog out? And what if the family that adopted him had children? "Can he be socialized? I mean, so that someone could adopt him?"

Dr. Bild shook his head. "That I don't know. Just avoid touching him for a while. He needs to get more acquainted with the idea of touch being related to pleasure, not pain."

That broke Rose's heart. She had been waiting all week to get the chance to pat Billy's fur and let him know he was loved.

When she got the bill for $290, she handed over her credit card, mentally calculated the balance and hoped she hadn't already reached her credit limit. She was relieved when the charge was approved. Then Rose approached Billy who was patiently waiting, a leash attached to him, ready for the taking.

He looked so sad, so pitiful, Rose couldn't help but kneel down before him and look at him eye to eye. She wanted him to know she was his friend.

Billy stared at her, then looked away, his tongue coming out to lick his chops. Rose continued to kneel before him, waiting for eye contact again, but he wouldn't make it. He only looked off to the side.

She couldn't stand it anymore. She wanted to touch him so badly, an aching rose within her. Surely, he would respond if she patted him.

She reached out and touched his sizable head, trying to stroke trust into him. The growl warned her too late. Sharp teeth sank deep into her hand, making her cry out in pain. There was no Billy within his eyes as his teeth dug further into her hand, shaking his head to get a better grip on her. There was only Butch. The Butch that knew nothing but abuse and felt nothing but anger. The pain of knowing that surpassed the pain in her hand, which she couldn't pry free from his mouth.

Within moments, she and the dog were surrounded by people in the clinic who were trying to help. One pair of hands grasped the leash, another produced a muzzle and another tried to free Rose's hand that was dripping blood on the floor. But the animal, his eyes narrow and glassy, wouldn't let go.

Through tears of pain, Rose tried to ignore those hate-filled eyes, but they burned deep into her soul, shaking every belief she ever had about every dog being able to be saved.

A leg suddenly shot out and kicked the dog's side. He squealed, like a baby being hurt, and let go. The muzzle went on, the leash tightened and he was quickly led away toward the back.

"Give him a sedative until we figure out what to do with him," Dr. Bild quickly instructed.

Rose grabbed her wrist, holding her injured hand before her. Blood was pouring from her hand onto the floor.

"He must have hit an artery in your hand!" the vet cried, running toward her. "Tourniquet! We need something to make a tourniquet!"

Everything was beginning to haze. Rose didn't even know when cloths and gauze were applied. She felt the cloth that was tied about her elbow tighten swiftly with precision. All the pain and all the blood she would gladly endure all over again if she knew Billy could be saved.

But his fate was all too clear. He would have to be put to sleep. Not just because he bit her hand. But because no matter who tried to help him, he would never learn the lesson of trust. She saw it in his eyes. In his angry, fearful eyes every human had a baseball bat.

❖❖ Chapter 21

Through Wind, Rain and Snow

One morning, not long after she had Billy put to sleep, Rose awoke only to find she couldn't get out of bed. Her body felt achy, wracked with chills and suddenly, she let out a whooping cough. Her head pulsated with pain and nausea threatened. No one was there to bring her a cup of hot, soothing tea or to get her breakfast. Wiggles was curled up at the end of the bed, lightly snoring, unaware of the fact that Rose had even awakened.

She quietly observed her dog, noting how peaceful he seemed, his sides rising and falling to the rhythm of sleep. She shook her aching head and let out a sigh. Wiggles reminded her of the duty she had. Sick or not, she couldn't stay in bed knowing that her strays hadn't been fed. She glanced out the window to see snow still falling though it appeared to be letting up. On the floor next to her was a pile of papers she had been studying on no-kill shelters that would take in any dog she brought to them. Unfortunately, the closest one she had found was a four-hour drive away and with all the snow coming down since yesterday it would be closer to five hours.

If she could get a local shelter to take more interest in what she was doing and promise her no termination dates, she wouldn't have to travel so far to be sure the dogs she rescued would be safe.

She pushed the covers off, ignoring her weak body that fought against rising. The night had been long and cold— only eight degrees—and she hoped that whatever food she delivered would help the strays through the horrible conditions.

Somehow she dressed and had a cup of tea. Then, summoning all her strength and still coughing, she went outside. The snow, which had been falling since the previous afternoon, had begun to taper off. She grabbed a large shovel and began digging her van out of the drifts. Her arms shook with each shovelful of heavy snow. The wind struck her relentlessly, making her job almost impossible, but Rose kept at it. She knew if she paused, even for a second, she wouldn't be able to go on.

Once she uncovered the wheels to the van, as well cleared the driveway, she tossed the shovel aside and headed toward the garage where she stocked most of the supplies for the dogs. Going to the far corner, behind stacked cans of dog food, she spotted the largest bag. Grasping the two corners of the forty-some pound bag of dog food, she dragged it through the garage, out through the snow and toward the van. She paused to open the van door and grabbed hold of the large bag of food.

Perspiration dripped down the side of her face. She shivered. *One swift swing*, she told herself. Just one and she would be able to get the heavy bag into her car. She stared at the bag one last time and yanked it high enough to hoist it into the van.

Suddenly, the bag ripped, spraying hundreds of brick-colored bits of dog food into the air, snow and van. Rose stood there for a few moments, unable to react. Had she not felt so awful she would have sworn at the bits of dog food on the ground, kicking them off to the side into the snow. Now, tears ran down her cheeks.

"Another bag," she said hoarsely, steeling herself and turning away from the mess. She trudged back toward the garage.

Taking hold of the ends of another large bag of dog food, she closed her eyes for a moment, praying for strength. She dragged it through the snow back toward the car and slung it into the back door. She sighed, grateful this bag didn't rip. She glanced at the back of the van to make sure there were enough plastic baggies she could pack food into once she got to Dalton City. "Thank goodness," she murmured, seeing them.

Luckily, driving was easier than expected. No more snow fell during her trip to Dalton City, making visibility easier. Her temperature, however, had risen considerably and she felt like she was driving in an oven.

Pulling the car off to the side of the road where she usually parked when she fed the strays, Rose unzipped her jacket and climbed out, thankful for the burst of cold air that hit her.

She opened the side door of the van and started the tedious job of filling bag after bag of dog food. When she had filled close to twenty bags, she paused and looked behind her, thinking someone was watching her. No one was there. She took some of the bags, closed the van door and made her way to the usual spot where she left the bags of food.

There were traces of food from the last feeding she had left and she smiled thinking about the animals who were no longer hungry. "I have to keep going," she told herself.

She knelt down and as she did, she had the funny feeling again that someone was watching her. Slowly, she looked toward the abandoned building that loomed directly across from her and started. A pair of large eyes were staring back.

She peered at it carefully. It was a fairly large, spotted dog that looked a lot like a dalmatian. She was surprised. There weren't too many pure breeds in this neighborhood. Mike would have pulled out his book and double-checked it, but she was pretty sure. And it was horribly skinny, just like all the strays seemed to be.

The dog continued to watch her and Rose had the sense that this particular dog came to this spot often, though she had never seen him or her before.

Rose rustled open a small bag of food, pouring a little into her hand and holding the rest in her other hand, hoping to bring the dog closer.

The dalmatian shifted from one direction to another, as if trying to make up its mind whether it should approach. Rose patiently waited, the cold further sucking out the heat she had earlier felt. Nevertheless, she was obviously feverish, her hands and body trembling as she continued to wait.

She watched as the dog sniffed the air and to her surprise, finally came over with no trepidation in its eyes or stance. It paused about a foot away, sniffed the air again and then moved forward just enough to stretch out its neck to eat from her hand. When that was gone, she smiled and pushed the open bag of food toward the dog.

Instead of eating more of the food from her hand, however, the dog snatched the bag in its mouth and dashed off toward the direction from which it had come. The dog disappeared at the left side of the abandoned building, the rustling and echoing of the plastic bag fading along with it.

Rose continued to kneel in the snow near several bags of food waiting for the dog to come back. She waited for about fifteen minutes, but the dog didn't return. Pushing herself to her feet, she realized she felt dizzy and nauseous, but she wasn't about to head back to her van yet.

Zipping up her jacket to her chin, she looked around trying to decide whether to go after the dog. Stray dogs are very territorial, she knew, but she had a nagging feeling the way that dalmatian had grabbed the bag and carried it away, that it was dinner for more than one.

Rose crunched through the snow and followed the trail of paw prints toward the back of the building. Pausing when she came to a crawl space where the paw prints

ended, Rose bent over and peered inside a broken window-
pane. All she could make out was darkness.

She wondered if she should crawl in after the dog, but
the opening was very small. Though she thought she'd be
able to crawl in, Rose feared she might have trouble getting out. She certainly didn't want to get stuck or trapped
inside when no one knew she was there. Suddenly, her
thoughts were interrupted when from somewhere deep
within the bowels of the building, came the sound of
scratching and yipping. She stood hunched over, listening
as the yammering of a few small barks continued. "There
must be puppies in there," she murmured. And the dog she
had just seen, running off with that bag of food, was without a doubt the pups' mother.

Rose backed away from window and bit her lip thoughtfully. When it came to a mother and her puppies, one had
to be careful, she knew. The mother was more than likely
to respond aggressively to protect her pups from danger.
Then again, Rose might scare off the mother. It probably
would then take the puppies to another area which would
result in a failure to save them instead of a rescue.

Perhaps she better leave them alone, Rose decided.
Slowly, she began walking back to the van. But as she
walked, she grew increasingly concerned for the dogs she
was leaving behind. What was the chance that a mother and
her pups could survive the rest of this harsh winter? The
odds were not very good.

She went to the van and gathered a few more bags of dog
food, which she left near the building's broken window in
the hopes the mother dog would find them. Feeding the animals and watching them to make sure they were doing fine
was all Rose could do at this point. She felt she could get
into the crawl space, but she wanted to have someone with
her just in case she ran into problems. She knew Mike
would gladly help her, but she wasn't sure he'd be able to
help her if she got stuck. Plus, it would make more sense
for the smaller of them to go in, but there was no way she
was sending little Mike into that crawl space alone. No, she
would keep Mike out of this dangerous rescue. This was

going to be tricky since she couldn't rescue the dogs then and there, but she vowed she would help them.

She returned to the van, feeling lightheaded again and turned up the heat. She had to go home before she lost the strength to drive.

Snow began briskly falling a short while into her drive, hazing and blurring the street before her. She knew she should have been driving down the main road since it had been cleared by the city's snowplows instead of back roads, but she couldn't see well enough to make the correct turn. And if she turned onto an icy patch, she knew she might just be sending her van sliding over a curb and into a building.

Just as Rose was reaching the end of the block that marked the beginning of the commercial section of one of Dalton City's western suburbs, she noticed something laying on the side of the road before her. She leaned toward her steering wheel to get a better look and eased her car to a slow roll and then to a stop. Whatever it was, it was already covered in several inches of fresh snow.

She pulled her van over as far as she could despite the poor road conditions, put it in park and got out. As she drew closer, she noticed a stiff, furry leg sticking out of the snow.

"Oh my God." She hurried over. A furry leg, black nostrils and pale gums were all she could see through the snow. That's when she noticed that some of the snow was bloodred. It was melting and mixing with the fresher snow into the side of the curb.

Since she left her gloves in the van, Rose took a bare, shaky hand and slowly pushed away the icy snow from around the dog's body. Although the long fur was wet and cold, warmth was floating toward her fingers from the creature. Its side was lifting and falling ever so faintly and had it not been for leaning over the dog and listening for the intake of its breath, Rose might have thought the poor animal dead.

Someone had hit the dog with a car and hadn't even stopped to take care of it. Tears came to her eyes as the dog let out a low whimper. It lifted its head at her touch and looked at her with pleading eyes that were in such pain, it sliced straight into Rose's heart.

Despite the dog being able to move its head, it obviously couldn't move anything else. Assessing the situation, Rose decided she couldn't risk lifting the animal for fear of causing it further injury. She was amazed that it was still alive and able to lift its head. A collar and a dog tag around its neck told her it had a home somewhere.

"I'm going to get a blanket for you," she whispered, scrambling to get back to her feet.

She hurried over to the van, grabbed one of the many blankets stacked inside and moved back as fast as her weakened body would allow.

Folding the blanket a few times to increase warmth, she gently placed the cover on top of the dog's soaked body. She stared at the dog in a state of helplessness and then looked back to the van, wondering what she should do. She couldn't just up and take the dog. What if its spine was damaged?

"Oh God," she half-whispered to herself, touching her head that was pounding away with pain. "What am I going to do?"

As the dog's whimpers began fading, Rose knew she had to act. In its frail condition and the temperature being as cold as it was, who knew how much longer it would last here on the street?

"I'll be right back, sweetie. Hold on."

Despite feeling unsteady, she hurried over to the van, pulled open the door and yanked out her purse. Digging around in her purse, she located her cell phone and pulled it out. Who should she call? Since she was just outside Dalton City, who would help her? If only Bob were around. If only she could call him for help. If only...

Focus, Rose. Focus.

She pulled an address book from her purse where she had written down the names and numbers of all the nearby shelters. She stared at the first number that jumped out at her. The Humane Society.

She didn't even know why she put that number in her address book. They were never of any help before. Heck, they had even blacklisted her. But as Rose's eyes ran across the names and addresses of countless other shelters, she saw most of them were hours away. Her eyes drifted back to the listing for the Humane Society that was located just on the other side of town. At most, it was a half hour away. If only, this time, they would help. But she was sure they would say no, especially since it was her.

She would have to call Dr. Bild instead, even though for him to send his emergency vehicle would cost her a fortune.

"Dr. Bild's office, this is Charlotte."

It was a voice Rose didn't recognize. "Are you new?"

"Yes. I just came on this week."

"Well, Dr. Bild knows me. My name is Rose Block. I bring a lot of neglected and abused dogs to him for treatment. I'm calling because I found a dog just outside Dalton City that was hit by a car. It looks pretty badly hurt. I didn't want to move the animal because I don't know the extent of the injuries, but I just can't leave it. I didn't know who else to call."

"You know we have to charge you to come out there. You should really call the Humane Society," the woman said.

"I know, but I just can't. I'll pay whatever the costs are. I can't leave this dog here."

"Okay, where are you? Give me two cross streets."

"Stockwell and Roscoe, about five minutes north from highway twenty."

"Okay, what I want you to do is make sure the dog is warm. I'm assuming because it was hit by a car that it's out on the street."

"Yes, it's out on the street, but I already put a blanket on it."

"Good."

"Is there anything else I should do?"

"Not unless there's profuse bleeding. Is the dog heavily bleeding?"

"No. I mean, there's blood, but the dog doesn't appear to still be bleeding. I think it's either stopped or slowed down or maybe the problem is internal."

"Okay. Now what I want you to do is stay with the dog so we can find you. Let me get your name and number. I'm going on break so I'll come with someone else. We'll be out there right away to help you."

"Right away?" Rose asked slowly, unable to mask her disbelief. No waiting? Just like that?

"Yes, of course. And your name and number where you can be reached? Are you on a cell phone right now?"

"Yes, yes, I'm on a cell phone right now," she stammered. She gave the woman her cell phone number. Even though Dr. Bild helped her whenever she brought a dog in, she had never received help out on the streets from anyone. She was shocked and relieved at how readily his staff was willing to come to her aid.

"Okay, Mrs. Block. I want you to wait by the dog and have your cell phone on you in case we call."

"Okay."

"We should have someone out there in about twenty-five minutes or less, depending on the road conditions. Hold on."

"Thank you. Thank you so much." Rose said, overcome with emotion.

As she scurried over to the injured dog and sat down beside it on the curb in the snow, Rose began to cry. They were a strange mix of tears, really, for she was heartbroken about the condition of the dog, while also filled with a sense of thankfulness and relief that Dr. Bild's staff would soon be out there to help her.

"You'll be fine," she assured the dog, adjusting the blanket on its trembling body. "Help is on the way. And until help arrives, I'll be right here talking to you and making sure you stay safe."

A half hour later, a small, white van with the words DR. BILD'S VETERINARY CLINIC in red drove up and parked behind Rose's vehicle. A woman and a man stepped out and pulled out a gurney from the rear along with items to treat the dog and ready it for the trip back to the clinic.

"Hi, I'm Charlotte," a young brunette with sparkling blue eyes said.

"It's okay. We'll take it from here, Ma'am," the man announced.

Rose nodded, pushed herself to her feet and wandered over toward a parked car which she leaned against. With each passing moment she felt weaker and weaker still. She pressed a cold hand to one of her heated cheeks, willing herself not to faint.

Charlotte and the man worked quickly, peeling away the blanket Rose had laid on the dog, giving it a tranquilizer, wrapping wounds and checking for broken bones and other injuries before slowly moving the dog with the help of the blanket onto the waiting gurney.

"Hey! Hey! What's going on there?" someone heading toward them from down the street yelled out.

Rose turned and saw a tall, blonde-haired man with a pockmarked face wearing black, moving into the street to where they were taking care of the dog.

"We got a call to pick up this dog," Charlotte said as she and the man moved the gurney toward the waiting van. "It's all taken care of though."

"Hey, that's my dog, you know," the man said, walking after them. "How much is this gonna cost?"

"That's your dog?" Rose called out in surprise, pushing herself away from the car.

The light-haired man turned and stared at Rose as if she were the one that had hit the dog with her car. "Did you call these people?" he asked accusingly, pointing toward the clinic's van.

Rose walked toward him, nodding. "I found your dog on the side of the road. It was a good thing she wasn't completely covered in snow or I wouldn't have seen her."

"Hell, I thought she was already dead. She should have been the way that car hit her."

Rose froze for a moment. "Do you mean to tell me you knew about your dog being hit and your didn't try to help it?" she asked in disbelief.

"Heck, yeah. I live right there." He pointed to one of the houses on the block. "That stupid bitch is always running out of the house and into the street. Yesterday, I went out to get the newspaper and she sprinted out and boom!" He smacked his hands together to demonstrate. "It happened just like that. This lady driving a Cadillac just did a hit and run, didn't even care to see what the hell she hit. I went out to look at the dog to see what happened, but seeing she wasn't moving, I figured she was dead. What was I supposed to do?"

"You mean you left her out in single-digit, freezing temperatures, bleeding, to let it face death on its own? It's a miracle the dog is still alive," Rose said in horror.

The man shrugged. "I didn't know how much it was going to cost me to get someone to pick her up off the street." He glanced toward the white van into which his dog was being put. "That's not going to cost me anything, is it?"

Rose passed a shaky hand alongside her face, afraid of what she might say to the man before her. As many times as she had seen it, as many times as she had lived it, never could she get used to the idea of people being so heartless, so uncompassionate. "I'll be covering the vet's bills," she calmly stated. "I'll just make sure that if this dog survives, she's going to another owner. It's obvious you can't or won't take care of her."

"Hey, that's fine with me," he said, waving her off. "It was really my ex-girlfriend's dog anyway. Two bitches if I ever saw them. My girlfriend never came back to get it, so I was stuck feeding the mutt and putting up with every damn squat. Hell, she was a pain in the ass, as far as I'm concerned. I've had pit bulls that were easier to take care of."

Rose swallowed the lump that had formed in her throat and walked away, forcing herself not to say another word. It was obvious this man would not be swayed by reason any more than he'd been swayed by the sight of a seriously wounded animal. Her energy needed to be put to good use making sure that this brave dog survived, not berating its ignorant owner.

Charlotte and her helper took the dog to the animal clinic. Rose followed in her own vehicle. When she arrived, she waited to talk to Dr. Bild so she could learn the dog's prognosis. Dr. Bild got right to the point.

"Broken bones, several dozen stitches, the onset of frostbite, loss of blood, not to mention the serious trauma her body was put through. We need to keep the dog here for a while," the doctor mused as he examined the dog.

"But she'll be all right, won't she?" Rose insisted.

The doctor nodded. "Yes, she will, but you might want to start thinking about placing her in a shelter about three weeks from now. I know how hard it is to place these dogs in a shelter. A no-kill shelter is what you need to find. Most shelters, including the Humane Society, have termination policies after so many days."

"I know," she replied. "I know all too well, Dr. Bild." The no-kill shelter she had found was full every time she called them, because of their no-kill policy. Openings in such wonderful places were so scarce, she knew she had to start asking for a spot now. "Thank you for all your help."

"Sure thing. Any more questions?"

She sighed. "Could you tell me about how much this is going to cost? As you know, I rescue a lot of dogs and it's so expensive," Rose said sadly. "I hate to complain, but it's hard."

The vet took a deep breath, releasing it with what Rose could only describe as fatigue and looked toward the open door. "Listen, Rose. I know you're going to keep bringing them in and bringing them in and I admire that. But I have a business to run here and two partners. Now, even though it is a business, animals are still a priority for me and I don't want to see you turning away from what you're doing. So, how about we strike a little deal here? I'll discount the total bill by twenty-five percent but only if you keep the amount of dogs per week down. Otherwise, I can't keep doing this."

"A discount? That's wonderful! Thank you, thank you so much!" she paused, all of the vet's words now completely filtering through her thoughts. "So, how many dogs a week are you limiting me to?"

He smiled. "How about three? I can't give you a discount or my time for more without it getting hairy."

"So what am I going to do if I run into more than three in a week?"

"I know you ran into some problems with the Humane Society in the past, but it really is a fine organization. They recently brought in new management which began implementing some new policies. In fact, I've talked to them about what you're doing. You should contact them again. I'm sure they'd be happy to help you. Like I said, the organization is going through some changes, getting rid of people, bringing new people in and I'm sure they'll be more understanding. You know, you should really ask about food, too. They give out free dog food now. I don't think I need to tell you that buying all that dog food is costing you a lot."

Rose fought against an oncoming cough, but couldn't keep it down. She whooped, her chest aching.

"And I really think you need to take better care of yourself, Rose. You look like you have the flu and you're been out in this freezing weather?" The doctor shook his head. "You need more people to help you."

"I know, I know." She coughed again. "But there are so many animals in need. Just early this morning I found a mother and its pups in an abandoned building. I need to go get them out, but I don't know how."

"Well, you're right to be concerned. You have to be careful. The only way to do something like that is trap the mother and then gather up the pups, but depending on how smart the dog is, that might be hard." He shook his head. "Just don't do everything yourself. Talk to the people at the Humane Society. Get help, Rose, or you'll burn out." He smiled warmly at her. "And then what will these dogs do? They'll have no champion."

Chapter 22

Humane Aid and Small Miracles

Gathering up her courage, Rose slowly walked into the office of the Humane Society and went up to the receptionist desk. "My name's Rose Block and I'm here to talk to Elizabeth Corey about animals I'm trying to help."

"Wait right here, please." The man got up and disappeared into one of the offices.

Moments later, he was followed out by a fiftyish woman with gray hair cut in a bob.

"So, we finally get to speak in person, Mrs. Block," the woman said, extending her hand to Rose. "It's nice to meet you. I'm Elizabeth Corey."

Nervously, Rose took the hand being offered and noticed her own was perspiring. She took a deep breath and let it out. "So I take it I'm no longer being blacklisted?"

Ms. Corey smiled and pointed toward her office. "Let's talk in there."

Ms. Corey closed the door, indicated Rose should take a seat and sat down herself. The two women looked at each other appraisingly for a few moments without speaking.

Rose was still in an uncertain frame of mind. All she could think about was whether this visit she had made to personally speak to Ms. Corey was worth the time away from her dogs.

"Mrs. Block, I know we got off to a bad start, but Dr. Bild has spoken admiringly about you. From what I understand," Ms. Corey finally said after picking up a pencil, "you work in an area that has no animal control, where animals are being not only starved, but neglected and beaten. You must understand that we get calls all the time from people needing our help. Some are reliable and some are not, but I have to say I've never heard anything quite like this."

Rose shook her head. "I know it's hard to believe. I don't think I would have believed it myself unless I saw it, which is why I need help so desperately. I can't keep up with all the work needed to help the animals in this neighborhood."

Ms. Corey nodded and leaned toward the desk to write something down on a pad of paper before her. "And what about your interests?"

"What about my interests?" Rose asked, unsure what the question was referring to.

"Why do you do this? There must be a reason. I come across very few people that are this devoted."

"Oh." Rose hesitated before answering. Not that she didn't know the answer to the question. She knew within her heart what the answer was, she just didn't want her answer taken the wrong way. "I do this because no one else is taking care of these dogs. When I first started out helping these animals, I found that help was scarce and difficult to find."

"It usually is. Now, what, aside from taking dogs from their owners, have you done for these animals?" Ms. Corey asked, writing something else down.

Rose suppressed a cough, then cleared her throat. "I've been feeding them, trying to get ahold of as many as I can to spay or neuter them so the problem of stray dogs doesn't multiply and trying to get them into shelters so they can be adopted."

Ms. Corey looked up from what she was writing. "It sounds like you have your hands full, Mrs. Block." She dropped the pencil onto the pad of paper. "Have you ever thought of becoming an investigator? One of the reasons we haven't been of much help is because we're in dire need of them."

"And what does an investigator do exactly?" Rose asked, shifting in her seat.

"More or less the same thing you're doing right now. Except for the feedings. And you'd have a set of rules to adhere to. An investigator doesn't resort to stealing, no matter what the situation. You'd have to put in some hours for certification purposes and take some classes and, with your passion for animals, I'd write up an excellent recommendation for you."

"No feedings. A set of rules. No dog st...no dog 'liberating,' no matter what the situation. Ms. Corey, that would mean most of the animals I've rescued would have died." She slowly shook her head. "I'm sorry, but I don't think I can be an investigator for your agency."

Ms. Corey nodded. "I understand." She picked up her pencil again. "In order for us to help you, however, you have to promise us that...." She paused, seeking the right words, then smiled at Rose. "...you'll refrain from breaking any laws. If you can make us that promise, we'll assign someone to that area."

Rose stared at the pad of paper Ms. Corey had been writing on. It had the words "investigator," "Dalton City," "strays" and "feedings." Rose could tell the woman was sincere and was patiently waiting for an answer. She needed the help desperately and if promising to refrain from stealing dogs for a while meant getting that help, she would make that promise. But that didn't mean, when the situation called for it, that she wouldn't step in to help a dog that needed her.

"If you assign someone to the area and they do what they're supposed to do, there won't be a need for me to take dogs," she truthfully responded.

Ms. Corey nodded. "That sounds fair. Here, take my card." She pointed toward the neat stack in a plastic holder at the end of her desk. "We're going to try to help you all we can. If we don't meet your expectations, you can call me personally."

Taking the card, Rose opened up her purse and carefully put it into her wallet. "Thank you. This means a lot to me. And a lot more to those dogs."

Ms. Corey smiled. "Is there anything else you wanted to talk about?"

"Yes," Rose quickly said, jumping at the opportunity. "Do you trap dogs?"

"Yes, we do on occasion."

"There's a mother and its puppies living in an abandoned building," she told Ms. Corey with an urgent tone in her voice. "With the weather so awful, I'm worried they're not going to survive."

Ms. Corey nodded. "I see." She picked up her calendar and studied it for a minute. "We can arrange something with Bart at the beginning of next week. He's good at trapping families. Is that soon enough?"

Rose nodded and let out a cough. "Thank you."

"Would you like a cough drop?" Ms. Corey plucked a box from her open drawer.

Rose shook her head. "Actually, I'm heading to the doctor after this. I can't shake whatever it is I seem to have."

"Well, I hope you feel better. We'll contact you as soon as Bart sets a date for the trapping. And Mrs. Block," she paused and met Rose's eyes. "I was wrong about you. You're doing wonderful work."

"Thank you."

Rose nodded, picked up her purse and, unable to stop coughing, she put a hand in the air as a means of saying good-bye. She was worried that her cough had grown worse and her head throbbed. Despite Ms. Corey's conciliatory words, Rose felt miserable as well as sick. She was supposed to be taking care of all those dogs, not herself.

When the doctor diagnosed bronchitis, he put Rose on antibiotics and other medications which made it impossible for her to drive. Knowing she couldn't step out of the house turned her earlier form of misery into near depression. All she could think about was the dogs. The poor dogs were suffering, because she had gotten sick.

Five days later, just as Rose was finishing her medications, Elizabeth Corey from the Humane Society called to tell her that Bart wanted to do the trapping for the following day. "Are you feeling well enough to go with him?"

The thought of saving the dalmatian family raised Rose's spirits. "I wouldn't miss it," she said hoarsely and readied herself for her first outing and rescue since she had saved the dog by the side of the road.

That night, an ice storm blew in. It was so fierce Rose could hear the windows rattling around her in protest. She stood at the picture window looking out on the street. Sheets of ice coated everything in sight. She closed her eyes and prayed that every stray of hers had found a place to hide from the storm. If it weren't for the horrible conditions of the roads and the fact that newscasters were warning people to stay inside, she would have taken her van out right then, looking for any creature in sight that needed food and shelter. If only Bob was there to help her. If only... She shivered and wrapped her arms around her body willing herself to keep her mind on the dogs.

Luckily, the next morning was clear and bright. In what Rose hoped was a sure sign of spring just around the corner, the temperature had gone up to forty degrees and the ice was melting. Rose drove to the Humane Society and Ms. Corey introduced her to Bart, the man who would be handling the trapping. Rose rode in the Humane Society van with him.

As they parked on the block, Rose looked across the street and cried out, "The building, Bart!" She jumped out of the van and rushed across the street with him following. "The building!"

Or what was left of it. The roof and most of the walls and ceilings of the second floor had collapsed heaping dirt and rubble on the first floor and basement. Loose bricks were scattered everywhere. "Oh my God! What about the dogs?" she cried out.

Bart let out a whistle. "Damn almighty."

"What happened?" she said again, shaking her head. She slowly approached the half-destroyed building. She was trying hard to keep herself from breaking down and sobbing. "I don't understand what happened."

"The ice storm," Bart commented, following her toward the site. "I'm pretty sure the ice storm did it. You hear about this stuff all the time. If the building's not very stable to begin with, all it takes is one good ice storm and it'll collapse under the weight. Luckily the entire building didn't go. Let's just hope those dogs found a way out or are still okay in some protected space on what's left of the first floor or the basement and there's enough air. They're smart, you know. I'm sure if the mother heard the cracking sounds of the walls collapsing she would have started pulling out the pups one by one."

"Oh God, what if they didn't make it?" The thought stabbed at her. If she hadn't been so sick, if she hadn't waited, if she hadn't...she ran toward the side of the building, determined to find those dogs.

"Hey, Rose! Wait up!" Bart called after her. "You need to be careful. The rest of the building might still cave in."

"I don't care. I have to get them out," she called over her shoulder as she kept running.

Rounding the building to get to the window, Rose slipped and fell onto a pile of bricks, her hands hitting hard against them as she went down. On her knees, hardly noticing her cuts, Rose pulled herself toward the opening that was at face level now, only to find herself staring at a boarded-off entrance.

Horrified by this new obstacle, Rose tried to push the wood in with her bleeding palm, but it didn't work. She pushed harder, frightening urgency filling her with each passing moment.

"Noooooo! Who did this? Who did this?" She hit her fist into the planks of wood uselessly.

"Are you all right?" Bart asked, running over to her. "What happened?"

"Someone boarded it up," she cried, hitting it again. "It was the only way out! How could they? How could they do such a cruel thing? Now the dogs are trapped inside. They have no way out!"

Bart helped Rose to her feet, then leaned over and picked up some nails and a few wood planks from the ground nearby. "Someone boarded it up pretty recently. I'm guessing just a few days before the building collapsed."

Rose grabbed the wood and flung a piece across the yard. "Why? Why would someone do such a thing?"

Bart shook his head. "Maybe it wasn't on purpose. Maybe the person didn't know the dogs were in there?"

"If I knew they were in there, someone else did too!" she exclaimed. "Oh God, it's too late. It's—"

He interrupted her. "We keep an axe in the van in case of fire and other emergencies. I'll go get it," Bart cried.

"Hurry! Oh God, I hope they didn't...Time is running out to save them!"

He nodded, raced to the van and was back in minutes with the axe, a flashlight and handful of dog treats.

"Give me the axe," Rose said. With adrenaline fueled energy she didn't know she had, she began swinging at the planks in front of her. When several splintered, she kicked at it with her boot.

Finally, she managed to cut a hole large enough for her to squirm through. She carefully climbed through and hoisted herself down to the basement floor inside. "Hand me the flashlight and the dog treats," she called out to Bart.

He handed them to her. She stuffed the treats in her pocket. "Do you want me to go in with you?" Bart asked.

"No, I can do this. I want to do this. Besides, I'll probably need your help more to get out of here."

Inside, at first, all Rose could make out was darkness. She switched on the flashlight and noticed the beam was very dim. *Oh, great,* Rose thought. *The batteries are practically dead!* She switched the flashlight off, knowing she'd need the light much more when she found the dogs.

She could barely see where to put one foot after another as she hunched over to avoid the partially collapsed ceiling. Half-crouching, she moved as quickly as she could. Suddenly, her knee banged into something hard. She winced. On the way in she had cut and skinned her knees right through her jeans. The wounds burned. The dust in the building penetrated her nostrils with every breath she took and made her cough. She gritted her teeth. She had to find those dogs.

As she crouched even lower to move under a fallen beam, she realized with some relief that since there was enough air for her to breathe, there was enough for the dogs, too. *They have to be alright*, she told herself. *That is, if they weren't injured by falling wood and bricks.*

As she continued searching for the dogs, her eyes slowly began becoming accustomed to the darkness. Suddenly, she heard a creak as the floor under her bucked. She lost her balance and went down hard, a sharp pain making her cry out. Sinking deep into the floor, Rose grabbed at her ankle. It hurt terribly. She hoped she hadn't broken it. She rested there for a moment, rubbing her ankle. She slowly rotated her foot then flexed it back and forth, relieved to discover it wasn't broken. She knew she had to get back up and move forward. Steeling herself against the pain in her ankle, she pushed herself off the floor and somehow continued on.

Within moments, she was deep in the bowels of the building, far away from any windows. It was darker than ever. She switched the flashlight on and shined it all around her. She gasped, feeling more scared then ever now that she could see more clearly how badly damaged the building was, how at any moment the ceiling or walls could cave in around her. She took a deep breath to steady her nerves, telling herself not to think about the dangers at hand and instead focus on finding the dogs.

As if something evil had read her mind, a roar stopped her thoughts as debris fell a few feet away. She coughed, gagging on the cloud of dust that rose. Her eyes stung and momentarily, she couldn't see. When her surroundings finally cleared, she aimed the dim flashlight ahead and inched forward until she found herself at a dead end: a pile of bricks, wood and other debris blocking what was once a doorway. Hearing scuffling, she paused and listened. Then she heard a muffled sound, one she couldn't believe. Rose waited breathlessly, trying to make out the sound. It seemed too good to be true—it sounded like yipping. Tears ran down her cheeks. She got on her knees and shined the flashlight between the bricks and wood.

And there they were. The mother dog and her puppies. Six beautiful puppies. Gently, Rose began moving bricks and pieces of debris to give the dogs an escape route from the small area in which they were confined.

Once she cleared a path, Rose dug into her pocket for a dog treat. "Come here," she gently prodded. The mother hesitantly moved forward as Rose deliberately inched back. Slowly, Rose made her way back to the small opening through which she'd entered the building. Dropping the biscuit on the floor for the dog, Rose quietly called through the window to Bart, "Give me a hand so I can climb out."

Bart helped pull her up and out through the window. "I was just getting ready to crawl in there after you," he said.

"I found them. They're all alive," she breathed. "I can't believe they all made it."

"Great work, Rose," Bart said, grinning.

"I got the mother to follow me back to the window," Rose said, motioning toward the small opening. "She's eating a large biscuit now. She should still be there working on it."

Bart moved to the window. "I've got to get in there and trap her before she heads back to her puppies," he said, disappearing into the building.

After the mother was taken out and placed in a cage, Bart carried out the yelping puppies two at a time. As he passed them through the window to Rose, she placed them carefully into a puppy carrier. Never had she been so relieved.

Standing in the Humane Society office, the dogs waiting in the van to be transported to a shelter, Rose desperately wished she had her own shelter. The Humane Society couldn't keep them and the no-kill shelter four hours away only had room for three of them. That left four dogs unaccounted for. One of these days, Rose promised herself as she signed for all seven dogs, she was going to open a shelter. And she wouldn't turn away any dog. One of these days, she would make it happen. But in the meantime, until she found just the right homes for these small miracles, her house would do just fine.

Chapter 23

Deadly Dogfight

"I don't know if you want to get involved in this—it's a dirty business," Royce said, scratching his beard. He'd been watching for Rose from the side of the road for several hours and hailed her van as soon as she drove into Dalton City.

"If it has to do with dogs being abused or mistreated, I do," she replied firmly.

He leaned toward the open window of the van as if he didn't want anyone to listen in. "Have you ever heard of a dogfight?"

She nodded her head. "Yeah, dogs fight. But what has that got to do with what I do? I never have any problems with the dogs as far as fighting goes."

"No, not that," Royce said. "I'm talking about a different kind of fight."

"What kind?" she prodded. "Tell me."

"A blood battle to the death between pit bulls using chickens or kitties for live bait. The guys who go to these fights bet on the most ferocious dog."

Rose bit her lip. It never occurred to her to try to stop a dogfight. She had always been concerned primarily with strays and abused pets. "Is this going on near here?"

"Yeah, about twenty blocks away in an old house near Young and Florence."

"How do you know about this?"

"Oh, you hear things on the street. I just thought I'd tell you. It's gonna go down in an hour or so, around six o'clock."

"Can you show me where the house is?"

"Yeah, but—"

"No buts. If you show me where, maybe I can get a look at those dogs. Maybe I can do something."

"Do something?" he repeated. "I thought you'd just call the cops."

"I haven't found them too helpful."

"There are some things you don't do. That's why I wasn't sure I should tell you. You can't just walk in on a dogfight and expect to be able to stop it. I think you should just call the cops. Hell, I would have, but I can't. They don't like homeless people 'loitering,' as they put it. But the guys who go to these fights aren't reasonable people that'll listen to you. We're talkin' mobsters, really shady people."

"Oh, so you've been to a dogfight?" she asked.

"Well yeah, when I lived in Indiana. Back then, it was just a bunch of drunks bettin' money. But like I said, that was back then. I hear the guys who run it now are from the mob and they're doin' coke instead of drinkin' beer and they probably got guns, too. From what I know, this is real shady business. Let the cops take care of it."

"I don't think they will," she said, shaking her head. "I once called about a dog being beaten and the cop laughed me off the phone. What's a dogfight to them?"

"I hear," Royce said, "dogfights are misdemeanors but the police don't enforce much in this state when it comes to animals. The thing the law is worried about is the gamblin' going on, not the dogfights. That's the illegal part, but somehow they never seem to catch 'em. If you give 'em a tip, maybe this time the cops can get 'em."

Rose looked at Royce for a long moment wondering what he'd been before he became a street person. "What if we looked into it?"

"We?" He threw his hands up in the air and turned away. "I knew it. I knew this wasn't worth the ten bucks. You're gonna get both of us killed."

Rose drummed her fingers on the steering wheel trying to release the tension building within her. If she could stop a dogfight she would. What did she need a cop for? Maybe she could sneak in and nab the dogs before the fight even started.

"Royce, we have to try to stop this. Get in the car and show me where the house is."

He hesitated. "I don't know. This isn't a good idea."

"Please," she said. "I'm going to try to find it with or without you. But, it would be much easier if you'd help me. Please."

He sighed. "I'm probably gonna regret this, but okay." He went around to the passenger side, got in and began to give her directions.

As she turned on the motor and hit the gas pedal, she jerked the wheel, the tires screeching.

"Rose, you crazy?" he cried out over the squealing tires. "Watch the ice on the road!"

"The streets are salted. Besides, we have to get there before they do," Rose insisted, pushing the gas pedal further into the base of the footboard.

"Hey, hey! Slow down!" Royce shouted, putting his feet up on the dashboard. "Young and Florence ain't that far from here!"

"For all we know, they already started the fight. There's no time for slow driving." Rose steered around a slowly moving car so she wouldn't have to slow down.

"Rose, we're not flyin' here. We're in a van!"

Rose looked over at Royce who was clutching the sides of the seat, staring in front of him as if he were looking into the eyes of death. She'd never seen anyone so panic-stricken in her life. "It's all right, Royce. Don't be scared. I'm a good driver."

"Are you?"

She shifted in her seat and brought down the speed, but only by ten miles.

"There's Young," he called out, and she paused at the stop sign. "Turn left," he said. "Florence should be a couple blocks up."

Moments later, they found the street and she parked in a deserted alley nearby. Rose reached into the glove compartment and took out some masking tape and tore off two pieces of a rectangular cardboard box she had planned to use as a makeshift cage.

"What's that for?" he asked, watching her.

"Just in case."

"In case what?"

"You'll see." She got out and asked, "Are you coming?"

He nodded. "Yeah, I'm coming. If I don't, you'll probably end up getting yourself killed. You're crazy, you know that?"

She shook her head. "Maybe I am. Come on."

She slammed the door and headed toward the front of the van. She quickly taped up her license plate with one of the cardboard pieces, then headed to her back plate and did the same.

"You're not only a crazy woman, you're a smart woman, too," Royce hissed at her. "I woulda never thought of hiding the license plates. Are you sure you were always an accountant?"

Rose laughed, then became serious, trying to focus on her surroundings. How would they get in? They had to be quick before anyone spotted them.

"Over there." Royce pointed toward a house across the street.

Immediately, her eyes located a bright light coming from the basement of a house.

Clapping, loud voices and barking confirmed the location. Now she had to figure out a way to get in there and stop the fight.

She walked toward Royce, who was leaning against the side of the van.

"What now?" he asked, pulling up the collar of his old, beaten up winter coat. "It's cold as hell out here. Don't ask me to stay out here as a lookout. I got frostbite a lot since I've been out on the streets and I ain't gettin' it again."

"There's gotta be a way to stop this." She bit her lip and looked around. If only—

"Hey, hurry up! They're gonna start!" a deep male voice yelled from across the street.

Rose took hold of Royce's arm, pulling him with her to the side of the van to keep them out of sight.

"They sound shady," she whispered.

Royce leaned over far enough to see the men. "Uh-oh. They look like trouble."

"It looks like we're dealing with regulars here."

Rose tugged at Royce's coat. "Come on. Let's follow them."

"Follow those guys?"

"Yes. We'll listen in on their conversation."

They crept alongside the parked cars on the street, careful to stay hidden behind the vehicles.

"Man, oh man, if Big Gus found out about our setting this up on our own we'd be fish bait," one of the men said.

"Yeah, no kidding," the other replied. "But it's not like he's gonna know. He's out in New York, remember."

"That was last week, you idiot. I don't know where the hell he is now."

They paused outside the building where the barking was coming from.

Rose and Royce moved closer.

"How much are you going in with this time?" the tall man asked. His leather jacket collar was pulled up, hiding his face from Rose's view.

"Two grand. Last time I tripled it. I figure if I can do that today, I'll be able to buy my broad the necklace she's been wanting and my old lady a dishwasher so she'll stop her complaining. And I'll still have plenty left over for myself. Let's hope this is good and bloody, so we can make lots of dough."

Rose gritted her teeth knowing the dogs were the ones that were going to get good and bloody. "I wish I had a gun," she hissed, straightening her back.

"I wouldn't be standin' next to you if you had a gun, Rose," Royce hoarsely whispered.

"I'm going in."

He grabbed her arm. "Nah, nah. Don't do it. They'll know you're not a regular."

"Wanna bet?" Rose crossed the street without even looking for cars and headed toward the back of the brick house. She could hear Royce scrambling after her.

"I can't believe you're doin' this," he whispered from behind her. "I feel like I'm in some James Bond movie."

She let out a nervous laugh. "We're not going to kill anyone or blow up a building, Royce."

They headed into a stairwell and followed it down to the basement. The door was shut.

"So, what now?" Royce asked, looking at her.

"We open the door." She reached out and turned the doorknob. It opened.

Cigarette smoke and noise greeted them. There was a crowd of men gathered at the far end of the room, laughing and hooting. The two they'd seen outside were collecting cash.

A crude circular fence with a brown-speckled pit bull in the middle of it was set against one of the walls. The dog paced inside the fence as if it was thinking of a way out. Back and forth, back and forth, its agitation rising and rising. Not that far from it was another pit bull, gray as a shadow, who paced like the devil in his underworld.

"So which kitty cat goes first?" a red-haired man cried, raising his hands into the air. "We got a white one, a black one and an orange one."

Shouts rang out.

Rose looked around and saw a cardboard box a few feet

away from her, holding three kittens. They couldn't have been more than four weeks old. Her stomach turned at the thought that they were going to be thrown between the two pit bulls as a means of starting the fight.

"Hey! Who are you?" someone suddenly shouted at Rose and Royce.

Rose caught her breath and Royce moved protectively in front of her.

The two men they'd seen outside swiftly approached them.

"Get the hell out of here," the dark-haired one sharply said.

Rose knew she had to think fast. Real fast.

"You can't let them leave. They've seen us and know what we're doin'. They'll snitch," the tall one said.

Rose's heart almost exploded in her chest. It sounded like they were going to kill them for walking in on their dogfight. But she couldn't let fear overtake her now.

Royce tugged on her arm. "Let's get the hell out of here before they slit our throats."

Rose didn't budge. "You can't do anything to me. Just try to. Gus would know right away it was you," she said, her hands clenched in tight fists. "I guarantee you wouldn't be doing this stuff anymore."

"You know Gus?" the tall man asked suspiciously.

"How?" the dark-haired one asked, putting his face close to hers.

Rose played it up as best she could. "Yeah, Big Gus is a friend of mine."

The man laughed crudely. "You aren't his type."

She didn't back down. She came this far, didn't she? "Yeah, from New York. I flew in with Gus the other day."

"So you know Gus. Good for you. Now get out of here." One of the men grabbed her arm and started pushing her toward the door.

"He told me about the dogfights. He told me I should check one out."

The man stopped pushing Rose toward the door and stared at her, not knowing what to make of her.

"Big Gus doesn't know about this fight, does he?" the man asked nervously.

"No, he doesn't know—for now. But what do you think he would say or do if he found out?" She kept her eyes locked on his, making sure her lower lip wasn't quivering. "BUT, I won't tell him anything if you let me take the dogs and the kittens. I'm part of an animal protection group. That's why I came. I don't care about the gambling. I just want the animals."

The man released her arm and swore.

Rose felt a new sense of power coming over her. They were really scared of this Big Gus. "Give me the animals and tell everyone to go home or you can deal with Gus."

"You're bluffing," the dark-haired man said.

"Am I?"

The two men exchanged glances.

"Jesus! Just take the damn animals!" the taller man cried, turning away. "Take them all and get the hell out of here!"

"I will." Rose turned to Royce, who looked at her as if she had just parted the Red Sea. "Go get carriers for the pit bulls," she instructed.

He nodded and shot out the door.

Rose approached the circle where a speckled black and brown dog was being kept. The dog stopped its pacing for the first time since she had arrived and looked at her. The creature looked exhausted. It looked somewhat starved, too. The dog would probably have torn the kittens apart just to have dinner.

"You can't take my dogs," an olive-skinned man said, coming up to her. "They're mine."

Rose looked at the man with disgust in her eyes and not a drop of fear within her. His face reminded her of so many abusive owners, ignorant and vicious.

She pointed behind herself. "Those guys are letting me take them. If you have a problem, talk to them."

With a cry, the man grabbed Rose, violently shaking her. Both pit bulls started wildly barking. "Those are my dogs! I paid for them and I'll be damned if you take 'em!"

"Let her go, Ted," one of them said, separating them "She's with Gus."

"Gus? How the hell did Gus's bimbo get in here?" the man cried. "I thought all this was quiet."

"Look, Ted, it's a freak thing. Just let her take the damn dogs. That's all she wants."

"You all right?" Royce asked, putting down the two cages he had gone for.

"Yeah, I'm fine," she said in a strong voice that concealed her fear. "Let's get the dogs in."

She reached out her hand to yank up the fence when the pit bull lunged. The metal was the only thing that kept her from being bit.

For the first time since she had begun rescuing dogs, she witnessed an unnerving viciousness in a dog.

The dogs' owner laughed. "Looks like we'll be having a fight after all."

Rose knew that neither she nor Royce could put the dog in the cage. "Put him in the cage," she told the man. "Put them both in the cages or Gus'll hear about this."

The man first looked at her and then at Royce standing next to her and swore. "They're my dogs, goddamn it. I don't see why I have to give them over."

"Get them in the cage, Ted," the tall man said.

The dogs' owner leaned over the fence, yanked out the dog by its neck as if it weighed nothing and shoved his hand beneath the dog's bottom to keep him from falling back in. Royce opened the cage and the man shoved the pit bull in. He did the same with the other, only with a bit more cursing.

No sooner were the dogs in than Royce took the carriers by the handles. Both dogs immediately started bashing their heads against the sides of the carriers, furiously barking and trying to get at Royce. But Royce didn't even flinch. He carried the dogs right out the door.

"Take the cats and get the hell out of here," the dark-haired man said, pointing toward one of the walls.

Rose hurried over to the cardboard box, knowing that her luck was going to run out at any moment and scooped

up the box. It weighed so little. Three soft balls meowed
and squirmed. She headed for the door.

"Gus isn't going to know about this, right?" the taller
man called after her.

She turned around at the door and looked at the group of
angry and baffled men. By the looks of them, one would
have thought she was walking away with their children. It
disgusted and terrified her at the same time.

"You got it," she said. She dashed out, feeling their
anger pursuing her.

Royce had just finished loading the two pit bulls into
the van. "Grab the cats and let's go!" she cried, giving him
the box.

They scrambled into the van and Rose fumbled to get
the keys into the ignition. Once the van started, she shifted
into reverse and backed out of the alley as fast as the vehicle would let her, hoping no one was following them.

Fifteen minutes later, with the pit bulls still wildly barking, Rose knew they had a problem she hadn't thought of
until now. The dogs would probably rip apart anybody or
anything that came near them. They were trained to do so.

"What are we going to do with the dogs?" Royce finally
asked.

She swallowed hard, the reality of the dogs' situation
hitting her. "They're going to have to be put to sleep. It's
not like they'll ever learn to trust anyone ever again."

She shook her head and drove toward the emergency animal clinic. The pit bulls banged against their carriers, causing them to rattle. Rose glanced back at them miserably.

"At least we saved the cats," Royce said, trying to make
Rose feel better. "And we're still livin.'"

She nodded, still trying to accept the pit bulls' fate. Why
was it that the dogs suffered most from their masters' cruelty? The bastard wouldn't spend a single day in jail for
teaching his dogs bloodthirsty tricks and yet the dogs
would be given the death penalty. It just didn't make any
sense.

The aching decision of having to put the dogs to sleep

weighed heavily on her heart. The dogs continued to bark and bang against the sides of their cages.

"Rose," Royce said softly, "You can't save 'em all."

"But I want to," she broken-heartedly whispered. "I want to."

❧ ❧ Chapter 24

Murder and Animal Control

As Rose drove through Dalton City late one afternoon it was as if the neighborhood was calling to her. *Make another stop. Bring us food.* She parked the van and slid open the side door. She started opening several bags, dumping dog food into one plastic bag after another.

When she had finished, she gathered them up and began walking along, tossing one after the other a few houses apart. A gunshot sounded, making her freeze. It sounded close, too close. Minutes passed and nothing happened. Suddenly, a police car sped past her down the street, out of sight. Rose was relieved to see the police were nearby, certain that whatever the problem had been, they took care of it. Still, she hurried back to the van, not wanting to learn the hard way that the shooter was still armed and loose.

Just as she grabbed the door handle to get into the van, she heard someone call out.

"Rose!" the young voice wailed. "Rose! I'm so glad you're still around."

She spun around to see a young boy racing toward her. "Mike? Is that you?"

He sobbed and threw his arms around her. "Grandma saw your van drive by earlier. She told me to see if you were still in the neighborhood."

"What's wrong? What happened?"

"They . . . they shot a stray. He's lying on the next corner, bleeding."

"Where?" she asked in horror.

He grabbed her hand and led her around the block to the corner. He froze and pointed to the sidewalk.

A dog lay there profusely bleeding from its gray, torn-up belly, staining what was left of the melting, dirty snow around it. A small crowd of residents stood nearby gawking at the scene.

Rose swallowed hard, trying to remain calm as she bent over the dog. With a wound like that there was no way she could help the animal. She knew the basics of first aid, but that wasn't going to be enough. This dog needed to be treated by a veterinarian immediately.

She knelt beside the dog and, with a shaky hand, touched his neck to feel for a pulse. She solemnly shook her head. No vet could help him now. Even though he was still warm, he was dead.

She stroked his soft fur as tears streamed down her face. How could someone do such a thing? "Who did it? Was it one of the neighbors?" she hoarsely asked, turning to Mike who stood beside her still crying.

"No. It was a . . . cop."

Rose snapped her body toward him, still blinded by her tears. "A cop? You mean to tell me a policeman did this?" she incredulously asked.

He nodded his dark head. "Someone wanted the dog off their front yard so they called the cops and they just came and . . . and I saw them shoot the dog."

"I don't understand. Why would the police do such a thing? Was the dog attacking anyone?"

Mike wiped his runny nose on his jacket. "No. He was just resting there."

"It's a cop's job," an older man commented as he broke away from the group of residents to approach Rose and Mike. "They do what they gotta do."

"What do you mean, they do what they gotta do?" Rose cried, rising to her feet. "Killing an innocent and nonaggressive animal isn't necessary for public safety."

The gray-haired man shrugged. "Them cops try to control as many strays as they can. There ain't any other animal control out here."

"So they kill them?"

He nodded. "Sure thing. Shooting them's the only way to keep them under control. Like everyone around here says, there's just too many of them." He looked down at the dog laying on the ground, shook his head and then turned away.

"I wish the cops would start paying attention to the real problems," Rose emotionally whispered. "People who rob and kill."

She shook her head and felt like crying again. "They won't shoot a killer, but they'll shoot a tired, hungry dog because it's in someone's yard? Does that make any sense?"

She turned to Mike. "We need to document this. Go to my van and get my Polaroid camera. It's under the front seat."

He nodded and hurried away.

Rose sadly looked down at the dog again, feeling sick to her stomach. Although there was nothing she could do to save this one, she wasn't going to let his death go unnoticed.

Within moments Mike was back with the camera. Rose stood up, looking through the lens at the stoic dog. She pushed down the button with quivering fingers. The rolling sound of the camera pushing out a picture followed. She put it in her pocket without even waiting for it to develop. It would seem she and her dogs had a new enemy—the police of all people.

"Let's give you a proper burial," she whispered.

When Rose got home that night she sat in the kitchen sipping tea and watching the golden retriever mix she had rescued and named Annie exchange playful barks with Valentine. Then Annie, whose leg was bandaged, limped toward Mutt and nuzzled with him in his bed. According to the veterinarian, her leg would be permanently scarred with the letters DW.

She sighed and got up. As she placed the dirty teacup in the dishwasher, she thought about Mike and the shooting he had witnessed.

She wanted to talk to Bob, but ever since the night Bob had followed her on that rescue mission weeks before, he hadn't returned home. She didn't know if he was on the road, but she feared it wouldn't be much longer before he walked through the door and started packing his things to leave permanently. She bit her lip trying to fight the tears that threatened to fall.

She felt terribly lonely. Lonelier than she had ever felt in all her life.

Walking out to the living room, Rose began pacing the floor only to stop and stare at the phone. She could continue to be proud or she could call Bob and tell him what had happened and her concern. Surely, despite their problems, Bob would understand the gravity of the situation and help her.

She strode over to the phone and picked it up but pressed it back down before she even heard the dial tone. She couldn't call him. He didn't want anything to do with her. He had said so himself. She picked up the phone again. Damn it, she had to call him.

She dialed his cell phone number.

"Yeah?"

"Bob, it's me. Rose. Please don't hang up. I really need to talk to you."

He sighed. "What do you want?"

"I was in Dalton City today where I usually go to feed the strays and a terrible thing happened."

"If you're calling me from a jail cell, all I have to say is I told you so. Look, I'm getting ready to go out."

Rose felt jealousy creep up on her. With who? Though deep down she felt certain he wasn't seeing someone else, it was the first thing that popped into her mind.

"I have a rig I have to drive to Bowling Green."

Although she was momentarily relieved to know Bob had been talking about trucking, not a woman, a new anxiety quickly surfaced. How was she going to handle this thing with the police? "Bob, today, one of the strays was shot."

"What? What do you mean, shot?"

She tried not to get too emotional. "The cops responded to a complaint about a stray dog being on someone's property and they shot him."

"You're joking, right?"

"I'm serious, Bob. Mike came and got me but the dog was already dead. Mike saw the dog get shot. He's devastated."

"I don't believe it. That's insane! Why would anyone kill an animal like that? Unless this one was vicious."

"It wasn't vicious. Mike said he'd been over that morning trying to get the dog out of the people's yard, but the animal was too exhausted. The police came and told Mike to go inside, but he watched from his window. He saw one of the cops shoot the dog. And, from what I'm learning, they do it a lot. It's being used as a form of animal control."

"Rose, this is serious. They can't go around shooting out in the open like that. Besides being cruel to the animal, it's downright dangerous to anyone in the area. Someone could get hurt."

"I know. I just don't know what I can do. I'm scared but this has to be stopped. We have to stop them. We have enough trouble from the locals without the police killing these dogs," she said.

"What's this *we* stuff?" Bob asked, his voice clearly strained.

Rose grew quiet. She had said *we*, hadn't she? She realized Bob had been on her mind since he'd left. Him and the dogs.

"Look, Rose, I think I made myself pretty clear. I trusted you and you lied to me."

"Bob, I'm sorry. I'm so sorry for the lies, but I would rather die than give up saving animals like Mutt, Wiggles, Lucy, Valentine and Annie. Just because the law says a dog is a piece of property doesn't mean it's right. And if you see an injustice and don't challenge it or do something about it, it will eventually grow into a huge problem and get more and more out of hand.

"Bob, I'm sorry. I didn't mean to hurt you and I lied when I said I don't need you. I do. More than I wanted to admit. But I feel like these dogs have only me."

"Look, I have to go and drop off this load. I'll call you when I come back later tonight."

"But what about the cops? What are we going to do?"

"Well," he said in a low voice, "I know someone who has a scanner.

Rose frowned. "A scanner? You mean, like a computer scanner?"

"No, a radio scanner. It lets you listen to police calls in Dalton City. I'll call my friend and ask him to listen in and tell you if there is any new information about the dogs."

"Thank you," she said.

"Rose." Bob's voice was sadder than she'd ever heard it.

"Yes?"

"I love you," he said softly.

"Oh, Bob," her voice broke. "I love you, too."

Silence filled the air.

"Rose," Bob stammered, "I've had a lot of time to think about all this since we've been apart. And...well, I've changed my mind."

"A-about?"

"About helping you." He sighed. "The truth is, I always knew you had a soft spot for animals so I shouldn't have been so surprised by this crusade of yours. You've been on my mind constantly since I left. I want to make you happy. And, if that means helping you with the dogs, then I will. That is, if you still want my help. Do you?"

"More than anything," she said softly. "I can't do this alone." She wished she could reach out and touch him. She ached to feel his arms around her. Just hearing those words made Rose the happiest she'd been in a long time. "Where are you now?"

"About halfway to Bowling Green."

"That's a long way from here." She paused. "Are you... are you coming home afterward?"

"I thought you'd never ask," he said, laughing.

Rose wiped away a tear that unexpectedly escaped the corner of her eye. She took in a deep breath as a smile spread across her face. They finally had reconnected. Just when she had given up hope, Bob was there to give it back to her.

❖ ❖ **Chapter 25**

"Shoot on Sight"

Early the next evening, Rose and Bob drove to Dalton City to feed the strays. As they passed a brick house, Rose noticed a small figure on the front stoop bent over a book. "Bob, pull over," she said. "I want to introduce you to someone."

As the van came to a halt, Rose turned to Bob. "He's probably still upset from what happened yesterday, so let's not bring it up. Just keep things light and cheerful." With that, Rose jumped out of the van. "Hi, Mike," she called with a smile. "I want you to meet somebody."

Mike looked up from his reading. "Hi, Rose." Though he tried to sound upbeat, his expression looked glum.

As Bob came around from the driver's side of the van and caught up with her, Rose said, "This is my husband, Bob. He's going to be helping us feed and rescue dogs from now on."

Mike's eyes widened. "Really?" he said hopefully.

"Yes, really," Bob replied firmly. "You can count on me."

Mike visibly brightened. Rose couldn't help but smile.

"Hey," Bob said suddenly. "I have an idea. We're about to feed the strays. Do you want to give us a hand?"

"Yeah, that sounds cool. Let me see if it's okay with Grandma."

When Mike disappeared into the house, Rose turned to Bob. "What a great idea. Thanks for suggesting it."

"Well, I just hope this helps get his mind off yesterday."

"I think it will," she responded.

A moment later, Mike bounded out the front door and down the steps. "It's alright with Grandma. She just wants me home by eight-thirty."

"No problem," Bob said. "Come on. Let's hop in the van."

Bob drove them a few blocks away while Rose gave him directions. When they got to the block past the field, she pointed. "Here's a good spot. Pull over." The van came to a stop. Rose looked out the window. "This is perfect. From here we can see what's going on in the field without being close enough to frighten away the animals."

Everyone climbed out of the van and went around to the back. "What's the story with the field?" Bob asked.

"It's a popular place for strays," Rose explained. "Packs of them live there. They hide in the brush and tall grass most of the day and then come out at night looking for food. It's a little too light for them to come out yet, but pretty soon it'll be dark enough. That gives us just enough time to get the food ready."

Rose opened the back door of the van and began getting the dog food and plastic baggies organized. Bob lifted Mike up so he could sit in the back of the van, his feet dangling above the pavement. Together, the three of them worked to fill dozens of little plastic bags with dog food.

When they finished, darkness had settled in around them. Rose suggested they get back in the van for a few minutes to wait until the dogs came out. "Once they come out, we'll know exactly where to throw the baggies so we don't waste any."

After a few minutes, they began to see dark, lanky forms moving in the field. "That's them," Rose said. "Let's see where they go and—"

The roar of two police cars racing by interrupted her. After they skidded to a halt only a few hundred feet away from the van, searchlights were positioned to illuminate the field.

"What's going on?" Rose whispered.

"I don't know," Bob replied, "but it doesn't look good. Maybe we should go."

Before Rose could answer, shouts came from the police officers now standing at the field's edge. Rose stared out the window and caught fleeting glimpses of stray dogs running from the bright lights, trying to stay hidden in the shadows.

Bob muttered, "What the hell are those cops doing?"

Rose shook her head. "I don't know. It almost looks like they're going to round up the dogs. But no one is carrying a dog pole, so they can't be planning to catch them. Unless... unless they're planning to..." She looked at Bob, her eyes widening with horror.

Without another word, Bob reached for a bag that was next to Mike on the backseat. Unzipping it, he pulled out a camcorder.

"What's that for?" Mike asked.

"You'll see," Bob said.

Bob put the camcorder in Rose's hands. "It may be too dark for you to get much of anything, but after what you saw yesterday, we'd be fools not to try to document whatever is going to happen here tonight."

"Oh, God, you're right. I can't believe this," she said, choking back tears.

"Oh no," Mike said, finally realizing the meaning of their words. "You think they are going to...to shoot them?"

"We don't know, Mike," Rose said. "We hope not, but after yesterday..."

Mike began crying. Bob got out of the driver's seat and sat next to Mike. He put his arm around the young boy. "Just don't watch. Don't look out the window. Close your eyes."

Rose tried not to let her emotions overwhelm her. She looked through the camcorder's viewfinder and began recording. Scrutinizing the area, she saw tails and lean bodies move in and out of the lights. Suddenly, a single gunshot rang out. Instinctively, Bob covered Mike with his body and Rose ducked down, trying not to drop the camera in the process. "Shoot on sight," a voice commanded. It was followed by the echoing of thundering bullets.

As much as Rose tried to remain focused, the rapid movements of the animals that rushed back and forth, howling in response to the bullets hitting them, made her quake.

Bob looked over at her. "Steady, steady," he whispered.

Dogs scattered leaving trails of red blood.

"I can't believe they're slaughtering those animals," Rose cried in a hushed manner, trying to get it all on the camcorder.

Mike lifted his head. "If only we could stop them," he whispered. Tears ran down his cheeks.

"This is the only way we can try to stop them," Bob whispered back. Rose, tears coursing down her own cheeks, steadied the camera, trying to remain calm.

Shots rang out again and again. That was when the horror of it all sank deep into her heart, her brain, her being. Dozens of dogs were being killed by the policemen. Then, as suddenly as it began, the hail of bullets ceased and there was only silence.

"I can't believe that just happened," Rose said in disgust. "If we were anywhere else, someone would have called 911 by now to report hearing gunshots. But not around here. Everybody closes their curtains and turns away no matter what the crime: gunshots fired, dog abuse, animal neglect..." She choked back a sob.

Still holding Mike, Bob reached up to the passenger seat and placed his hand gently on her shoulder. "We're going to see that they are held responsible for this, Rose."

Mike pointed out the window. "What's happening now?" he cried. A small orange glow emanated from the farthest corner of the field. Slowly, the glow grew brighter until crackling flames licked at the shrubs and tall grasses. Smoke and the smell of burning flesh assaulted them.

Rose looked at Bob and Mike. "They're destroying the

evidence so no one finds out what they've done here." She turned away, her anger mounting. During the past months, she had realized how difficult the world was for abandoned creatures, but it wasn't until now, witnessing the shooting and burning of innocent creatures in a vacant field, did she realize the depths of human beings' cruelty.

Mike was weeping.

"Don't worry, Mike," she said, a cold edge in her voice. "This time they won't get away with it. I promise you that. Bob and I will take care of this first thing tomorrow morning."

Mike dried his wet cheeks on his jacket sleeve. "Can I come tomorrow?"

"Sure. We could use your help. And," she locked eyes with Bob, "we'll need all the witnesses we can find."

Early the next morning, Rose and Bob stopped at the post office and mailed the videotape to the local television station, explaining in a cover letter what had happened. The quality wasn't great so Rose didn't expect it to be shown on the evening news, but she hoped it would motivate the station to do an investigation of the situation and uncover things she couldn't. She kept her fingers crossed as they left the post office to pick up Mike.

Less than an hour later, Rose, Bob and Mike hurried up the front steps of the police station. In her pocketbook were the Polaroid pictures. The dead dog shot two days earlier lay in the back of the van wrapped in blankets and several layers of plastic garbage bags. She had intended to give it a proper burial, but then decided the duty belonged to the officer that pulled the trigger. The thought of that dead dog, shot for no reason, propelled Rose faster toward the main desk where an officer sat.

"Can I help you?" the man asked, getting up.

Rose withdrew the picture she had taken and placed it on the counter. "Please look at this."

The cop leaned over and stared at the picture as if trying to make out what it was. "What is this?" he asked.

"It's a dead dog," she calmly replied.

"And?"

"And I'm not leaving here until this is looked into."

He stared at her, as if considering whether he should take her seriously. "What exactly do you want me to look into?"

She met his challenging gaze. "The fact that one of your fellow police officers is responsible for this."

"What are you talking about?"

"I'm talking about the way Dalton City police officers respond to animal control problems by shooting innocent and defenseless creatures without first making an effort to remove them from the premises."

"Are you serious?"

"Very serious."

He sighed, leaned back and yelled over his shoulder. "Frank? Ron? You wanna come over here?"

Within moments, two other officers approached the counter.

"Yeah?" one of them asked.

"This lady here says we'd better look into this." The officer picked up the photo from the counter and handed it to the younger man.

He looked at it. "What's this?"

"A dead dog," the officer responded.

"Yeah, I can see that, Rich. But what's this about?"

"Supposedly," the officer offered before Rose could say anything, "one of our guys shot the dog without doing a proper animal control procedure. Whoever it was just went and shot the dog dead, just like that."

"That's ridiculous. Who the hell would do something like that?" The officer handed the photo to the third cop that stood behind him.

"So, what do you want us to do?" one of them finally asked. "I mean, what's done is done. The dog's dead."

Rose crossed her arms to keep herself from shaking. She had never confronted three police officers before, telling them what to do. "The dog's body is in my van wrapped in some blankets and plastic bags. I want you to take the dog and find out whoever did this to him. Then I want you to have the person responsible bury the dog properly."

"What!" All the officers cried out almost at once.

"One of your people shot this dog because it was on someone's property, then just left the dog out on the street dying, for everyone to see. Including this little boy." Rose pointed to Mike who stood off to the side, his eyes still red and swollen from all the crying he had done in the past two days. "If you don't feel sorry for the dog, feel sorry for this child who had to see it. And from what I saw later, that's not the worst thing that happened."

"So you're saying one of our guys shot this dog?" the gray haired, heavyset officer carefully asked.

"That's right and if you don't take care of this problem, not only am I going to write to the state authorities, I'm going to make sure every newspaper gets hold of this picture."

The officers looked at each other, then at her.

Rose did the only thing she could to make them understand. "There are laws against this sort of stuff."

"So you want us to take this dog out of your car and lay it out in our office until we look into this?" the youngest officer asked, rounding the counter.

"I simply want whoever did this to bury him. Maybe it'll make whoever's responsible think twice about killing an animal. Clearly, this photo hasn't had much of an effect on you, so why would it effect any other officer? But maybe seeing all the blood and gore on the dead body will do it."

"If it's one of our guys, like you say it is, what makes you so sure he didn't act in self-defense?"

"Like I said, this boy witnessed the whole thing. And they didn't stop there," she said. "They shot more dogs the next night."

Rose pointed toward Mike. "The boy, my husband and I witnessed it and recorded the scene on videotape."

"Okay, okay, we'll take care of it. If it's one of our guys, of course we'll take care of it." The cop sighed. "Go ahead and bring in the dog."

"Mike and Bob, can you come with me?" she asked as she started out. "We'll be right back," she called.

When they reached the front door, Rose turned to Mike. "Wait here. We'll need you to hold the door open."

She strode to the van. Opening the door, she and Bob carefully took hold of the wrapped body and hoisted it up and out of the van.

Mike held the front door open for them while they carried the dog inside.

Two of the officers took the wrapped dog from Rose and Bob and carried it toward the back of the station.

The tall one soon returned. "We'd like to keep this picture for evidence."

"Sure," she said without hesitation and started to leave.

"Do you have any other pictures of this?" the heavyset officer asked.

"No," she said. "Come on, you guys." She took Mike's hand. As they walked away, she turned back. "By the way, I've sent the videotape to a local television station."

"Start cleaning up this mess," Rose heard the heavyset officer say as she, Mike and Bob walked through the front door. "Somebody's in deep shit."

When they reached the van, Rose turned to Bob. "I pray to God this will make a difference."

Bob embraced his wife. "I think *He* wants you to make the difference, Rose, and I believe you're going to."

❖❖ Chapter 26

Cruelty Strikes Home

Bob's words soon proved true.

One late afternoon the following week, Rose was driving only a few blocks from her home when she saw a man dragging a puppy on a leash across the street. She eased her foot off the gas pedal, slowing the car to get a better look. The young dog struggled against the leash, paws scraping against the pavement. She could see the puppy gagging and frothing at the mouth but the man just continued on yanking the leash with each step.

"Damn him." Rose pulled the van to the curb and jumped out.

"Hey! What are you doing? Can't you see he's choking?" she cried, approaching the man. "You're choking the poor dog."

"I wouldn't be if she tried walking," the man replied, pausing for a moment. He looked down at the pup and yanked on the leash again. "The stupid mutt won't walk."

Rose knelt beside the puppy and took hold of the collar. It was so tight it scraped the skin raw around the dog's tiny neck. The puppy was wheezing not only from being pulled along but from just wearing the collar. "You have to loosen the collar," she said, undoing and adjusting it properly.

The puppy hung its head as she touched it, never once looking up. It was only a baby, perhaps five or six weeks old. The little creature was clearly not ready for leash training. She tenderly scooped up the dog.

"She should be carried. She's too young to be dragged on a leash. You should paper-train her first." She held the puppy out for the man to take.

He stared at her as if she had just insulted his entire family, his face beginning to redden with anger. "It's got legs, don't it?" he cried, grabbing the pup from her. "She'll walk!" He dropped the dog to the ground. A yelp escaped from the pup.

"She's just a baby!" Rose cried, kneeling again beside the dog. "You have to treat her like a baby."

"I'll treat her any way I want to. You get back into that van of yours and mind your own damn business." He yanked at the puppy again.

Rose watched in disbelief as the man hurried on his way, the animal struggling and whining behind him. She got up and hurried back to her van.

She watched them, the puppy's little legs trying desperately to keep up with the man in front of it. "If that's not abuse, what is?" she murmured to herself.

When the man turned the corner, Rose pressed down on the accelerator and drove down the block, following him.

"Just try to get away," she quietly challenged him. "Just try."

He turned another corner, then headed toward a house which she assumed was his. She kept her distance but observed him as best she could, wanting to know what he was going to do with the puppy next.

He leaned over, picked up the dog and paused before the porch stairs of a blue colonial house. He knelt, opened the little lattice door leading beneath the porch and shoved the dog in, keeping one hand on the leash. He tied the leash in swift, thick knots, making sure with each knot that it was tight. Then he rose, went up the steps, unlocked the door and went into the house.

Rose would have taken the puppy then and there, but knew it wasn't a good idea. The man might call the police and after the shooting incident, she couldn't afford to get involved with the police any more than she already had. She had to keep a low profile, at least for a little while. She drove home knowing she had no choice but to go back when it was dark.

"Hi Bob. I'm so glad you're home," Rose said, walking into the living room and seeing her husband. "I need your help. Or, rather, there's a puppy that needs our help." She told him what she witnessed on the street and how the dog was kept tightly tied under the front porch all night. "It's supposed to be pretty cold tonight and it's only a puppy. It could die from exposure."

"Where on earth do you find these dogs, Rose?"

She sighed. "They seem to be everywhere I look. So, can you help me?"

Bob smiled. "Sure. But we're not keeping it, are we? I mean, we've already got six dogs and two cats in the house."

"What's one more dog, Bob?"

He sighed. "Yeah. What's one more dog? As long as we agree that seven dogs is enough. We have to find shelters for the rest of them from here on out. Promise."

She grinned. "I promise. Seven and not a dog more. Shelters for the rest," she agreed.

"So, how exactly are we going to help this puppy?" he asked, looking at her. "We're not stealing it, I hope."

"No, we're not stealing," she corrected. "We're rescuing. I know taking them makes you really nervous, but when it's over and a dog which was in jeopardy is safe, you feel wonderful." Rose paused. "It's dark enough to do it now. Please come with me. I can't bear to leave the little pup out in the cold a moment longer than necessary."

"You should write a book about all this, you know that?"

Bob drawled, grabbing his jacket and slowly pulling on his gloves. "Okay. I'm coming. Let's go."

"You still have that pocketknife in your jacket pocket?"

"Check."

It took them only a few minutes to reach the house—a blue colonial in the well-kept neighborhood. A dim light shone behind thin organdy drapes in the large picture window.

"I'll do it," Bob said, frowning but determined.

She smiled as he got out of the van. It felt good knowing she really had a partner at last.

She watched him crunch along the frost-covered lawn and move toward the lattice porch. He knelt down, pushed open the little door and crawled in.

"Please don't bark," she prayed. "Please, puppy, please don't bark. It's too quiet of a night."

Her eyes watched the window above the porch, hoping there would be no movement, no one peering out. Minutes passed and Bob still hadn't come out with the dog. She leaned forward to get a better view, wondering if the dog was still there. "Come on, Bob. How long does it take to cut a leash and grab a puppy?" she said aloud.

Just then, Bob emerged from beneath the porch, holding the front of his jacket cradling something small. He had the puppy!

Her elation, however, quickly turned to horror as the front door swung open and the shadow of a man stepped out onto the porch. Her pounding heart nearly exploded. There was no mistaking the shape of that long object in his hand—it was a shotgun.

"Bob, run!" she screamed, trying to shove open the door for him. "He's got a gun! Run! Run!"

A shot rang out. Rose jumped, her scream frozen in her throat. "Bob!"

Bob jumped into the car just as another shot rang out, grazing the door. Rose hit the gas. She didn't slow down until they were several blocks away. And even when the car slowed, her pounding heart didn't.

"Are you all right?" she finally asked, looking over at him.

"Barely," Bob replied, shifting in his seat. "I wasn't expecting to be shot at tonight."

"I didn't know he had a gun."

"Well, we know now," Bob said.

She gripped the steering wheel hard to keep her hands from shaking. "Are you all right?" she asked again.

"Yes, Rose. You asked me that already."

"I...did?"

"Yes, you did. Now breathe. Don't pass out on me behind the wheel. We've got to get away from that house as quickly as possible."

She took in a deep breath to steady herself. "Oh God. I can't believe that guy actually came at us with a gun. I didn't know he had one."

"You said that already, too."

She let out a shaky laugh and looked over at Bob.

He was smiling, despite everything that had happened. He leaned over and kissed her on the cheek. "I love you, Rose. You know that? Dogs and all."

She smiled back. "And I love you, Bob. Let's go home."

In the driveway they surveyed the damage to the van. "I can't believe that jerk hit my van," she said, putting her finger into the hole on the side of her car. She turned to look at Bob.

He was cradling the puppy. "He was determined to hit something. It's a good thing it was the van and not one of us."

Rose nodded, agonizing thoughts still running through her mind. What if Bob had been shot? What would she have done? It was almost too horrible to think about.

"You've got that intense look on your face again," he said. "You're not planning to steal another dog tonight, are you?"

She shook her head. "I was thinking how much you mean to me," she said lightly, trying not to cry.

He laughed. "That goes two ways. Now let's get this gal into the warm house before someone sees us."

Rose smiled and nodded. He took her arm with his free hand and they headed for the front door and opened it.

As they closed the door behind them, Rose said, "Let's find a spot for her in the kitchen and make some hot chocolate to celebrate saving her."

"Sounds good."

Rose put water in the kettle for hot chocolate and turned on the burner.

"Whatever dogs you rescue from here on out go to shelters or good homes. Not our home. Remember, you promised," Bob said.

She grinned. It was hard to believe that she had seven dogs in her home. "I got it, I got it. What about the cats? You think they'll want to stop at seven?"

"The cats are co-conspirators," he laughed. "Look at Peaches snuggling the new addition." He bent down to pet them both and nuzzled them with an affection Rose had never seen him have for animals before.

"Oh, so now you're an animal lover?" she teased.

"You sure as hell made me one."

Just then, Annie, Mutt, Wiggles, Lucy, Valentine, who was still moving slowly, and Pepper, one of the dalmatian puppies Rose had saved from the abandoned buildings, came in barking, wagging their tails behind them. They sniffed their new housemate and one by one, gave their tail-wagging approval.

Rose stirred the two cups of hot chocolate and set them on the counter.

Resting her cheek against her husband's chest, Rose felt his warmth fill her heart. A peace she hadn't felt in a long time took hold of her. This was how life was supposed to be. A "job" she really loved, a house full of pets and a loving husband whom she adored. It was like a sweet dream come true.

At that moment, the phone rang, interrupting her moment of newfound peace.

She raised a curious eyebrow. "I wonder who that could be?" She hurried to answer the phone.

"I bet you, oh, I don't know, ten dollars it's either Mike or Royce," Bob called after her, laughing.

"Hello?"

"Hi, Rose. It's me, Rick. I'm returning your call from the other day."

"Rick!" she exclaimed, happy it was her former boss. She had been waiting all day to hear from him. "Thanks for calling."

"So, why did you call?" he asked expectantly. "Don't tell me you want your job back?"

She laughed. "No. I was calling to see if you had any clerical positions available."

"For you?"

"For a friend. His name's Royce. He really needs a job and I thought who better than you to give it to him."

"Clerical work, huh?" There was a pause. "Yeah, I think I have something. Nothing big, though. It'll only pay minimum wage or maybe a little better."

"That's great!" She gave Bob a "thumbs-up" sign, excited. "So you're going to give him a job?"

"He still has to interview."

"You'll give him the job. I know you will."

Rick laughed. "With you as a reference, I probably will." He paused. "We all miss you at the office, Rose. Tell Bob, your girls and your dogs hello."

"I will."

"I'll call tomorrow and set up that interview."

"Thanks, Rick."

"Take care."

"Bye."

Rose beamed as she hung up the phone. Royce was going to be employed. She had a feeling this was going to change his life. He deserved it.

"So Royce is getting the job?" Bob asked.

She nodded. "It looks that way."

"And what about Mike? Your little helper?"

Rose smiled. "He's got some time before he has to get a job. But I have a feeling that boy is going to be a veterinarian when he grows up and I'm going to help him."

She handed Bob the cup of hot chocolate. "To us," she said raising her own cup and touching his.

"And the doggies," he added.

Chapter 27

An Animal Lover

One brisk spring Saturday morning when Rose went outside in her jogging suit to get the newspaper, she noticed a small Shetland sheepdog sitting on her front yard.

Rose slowly walked down the porch steps, leaving the front door open behind her. She stared at the white and tan dog, wondering where it had come from. It didn't take her long to figure out this dog, like the ones in Dalton City, needed her help. Its unkempt coat and scrawny appearance spoke of neglect. Amazingly, she didn't have to drive around to find this one. This one found her.

She glanced toward the house, wanting to call out to Bob, but was afraid she'd scare the dog away. Maybe she could lure the dog through the gate into her backyard and shut her in until she could figure out what to do with her.

"Come here," she cooed, bending over and wiggling her fingers to draw attention. "Come here."

The sheltie sprang up and ran toward the side of the house, disappearing.

Rose took the opportunity to call out to Bob. "Bob!" she

cried through the open front door. "Bob! Get a leash! Hurry!"

She then ran after the dog. Rose found the sheltie sitting before the garage door, trapped between her house on one side and the neighbor's fence on the other.

"I'm not going to hurt you," she said softly. "Do you have a name?" She found it always put a dog at ease if she had a name that she could keep repeating, so that it could become familiar with what she was saying. Often, neglected and abandoned animals never had anyone speak to them, except in an angry manner for something they had done or to get them off someone's property.

The way the dog was sitting told Rose it was a female. The first name she could think of was Jamie. "Jamie," she said, shifting closer. She even looked like a Jamie, it being a Scottish name. "I'll call you Jamie, all right?"

The dog yipped, as if agreeing.

"You wanted a leash?" Bob asked coming up from behind.

Rose looked over at him and seeing the leash in his hand, reached out and snagged it. "Stay where you are," she warned him, "you'll scare her."

She heard a sharp intake of breath and looked over her shoulder at Bob. He had a strange look on his face and was staring wide-eyed at the Shetland sheepdog.

"Bob, what's wrong?"

"Uh, nothing. Nothing's wrong. I just think the dog's already scared," he said nonchalantly.

Unsure why Bob reacted the way he did, Rose decided to let it go for the moment. She slowly stepped toward the dog, leash ready. "Come here, Jamie."

Jamie began frantically moving from one side of the garage to the other, contemplating escape, but seeing no means. She whined at Rose and Bob, as if telling them in her own language how scared she was.

"I think you should call animal control," Bob said agitatedly. "It's obvious the dog's scared. Don't put her through this. Animal control can trap her in one sweep."

Rose thought about it and sighed. He was right. There

was no sense causing further fear in the dog and a leash certainly wasn't going to protect her should it fight back.

Stepping back, she stuck out her hand, holding out the leash for Bob. "Take the leash and stand guard. I don't think she'll try to go around you or she would have done it by now, but watch her so she doesn't get away. I'll call animal control and make sure they take care of her."

When animal control finally arrived, Jamie not only exhibited fear toward humans, but sheer terror. Rose sadly wondered, as she helped force the dog back toward the side of the house, what happened to the sheltie to make her growl, yelp, plead, bark, snap and howl at the advance of a human.

They finally took hold of her with a snare. The dog crouched and submitted as if she were about to be whipped for all the resistance she had earlier exhibited. The animal control officers dragged her all the way down the walkway, into the street and to their van, her nails scraping the pavement every bit of the way.

Rose watched as Bob walked up to the animal control van and peered through the window inside at the sheltie. He put his forehead and a hand against the window. She watched in wonder as her husband traced his hand back and forth on that window, communicating to the dog inside.

A man stepped out from the van and said something that made Bob nod and step back. The man got back in the van and drove it away, but Bob continued to stand there watching the vehicle until it disappeared. He had been acting strangely since he first saw Jamie. Rose sensed something was bothering her husband.

"Are you all right?" she asked, coming toward him.

He was quiet for quite some time before turning to face her. "That dog needs a good family," he said, his blue eyes meeting hers. "I don't want her in shelters waiting weeks and months trying to get adopted."

Rose gently smiled in understanding. "She'll be put in that no-kill shelter up at Foster Lake."

"That's not good enough," he insisted, waving a hand. "We have to find her a home now or she'll never make it."

"But Bob, aside from all the treatments she's probably going to have to go through, she'll need to be socialized. And that takes anywhere from seven to eight weeks. You can't stick her in a home just like that. For all we know she might be aggressive and bite someone."

Bob stuck his hands into his jeans pockets and shook his head. "That dog's not a biting dog. I could see it in her face, her eyes. That dog looked at me and told me everything I needed to know."

"Yes, well, I thought Billy wasn't a biting dog, either. Remember? I told you about him." She held up her scarred hand, reminding him and herself. "I wish things would work the way we want them to, but there isn't an organization out there that'll put a dog up for adoption until they know the animal is socialized. And as much as I hate to admit it, she might not be adoptable. You saw how scared she was of people."

Bob took a step closer and leaned in until she could smell the coffee on his breath he'd been drinking with breakfast. "Are you going to tell me you're going to just let this take care of itself?"

"Bob, please," she tried reasoning. It wasn't like this was easy for her. She did what she could. "I've been at this a lot longer than you have and I really don't think it's fair for you to assume that I—"

"Fine. If it's not adoptable, then we'll take it. This dog comes to our doorstep looking for help and you're just going to send it off to some shelter?" He animatedly shook his head. "I don't think so. I think the Lord himself guided this dog to us. You don't think it's a coincidence this dog was sitting in our front yard staring at our house? Listen to me, Rose. I don't care what we have to do to get that dog back, but we're gonna get it. And if it means we're going to have eight dogs, instead of seven, then so be it. That dog spoke to me. Do you understand? She spoke what might as well be words and she needs more than physical treatment. She needs our emotional support."

Rose stared at her husband in astonishment. She never thought Bob would connect with any dog so quickly. "Do you want to tell me what happened out here?"

"I know it's silly, but remember the dog I told you about? The dog I had when I was a boy?"

"You mean the one that was run over?"

He nodded and scratched his head. "Well, she was a Shetland sheepdog, just like this one."

She smiled, understanding Bob's strong feelings about Jamie. This wasn't just about a stray. It was about a very special animal from his past. Just like she had the memory of her kitty, Valentine, forever locked in her heart, Bob would have the memory of his Shetland locked in his.

For that reason alone Rose would do whatever she had to do to get Jamie back. Besides, Jamie was the first dog to ever come to them asking for help. Rose couldn't turn away such a miracle that made her love for dogs also her husband's.

"Once she's treated, we'll find her a home," she promised. "And if we don't, she can stay with us and be the omega dog."

Bob kissed Rose's cheek, a smiled forming on his lips. "Let's make sure of that."

Bob visited Jamie at the shelter several times a week when he wasn't on the road, making sure her treatment for heartworm was going well. He wanted to make sure the shelter was doing a good job socializing her and asked to play with her himself, giving her as many treats as she would eat from him.

Indeed, Jamie had found her way to Bob's heart. Each night before he and Rose went to bed, he said the same prayer for the dog.

"God, help her learn to be trusting of humans so she can get out of there."

Rose did her best to keep up with Jamie's progress for Bob when he was on the road, while also feeding the strays, but Rose knew she couldn't keep at it for much longer. Foster Lake was a four-hour drive she often didn't have time to for.

Jamie was finally ready for adoption and Bob made it clear he wanted the dog to come home with them. From the time Rose had first seen Jamie sitting on her front lawn, to that day, she couldn't believe the changes the dog underwent. It went from being a skinny, submissive and scared dog to being a well-proportioned beautiful dog that happily greeted whoever came toward it. And it only took six weeks.

As Rose watched Bob snuggling Jamie against him, she noticed Jamie's little head sneak beneath Bob's arm to look at her. And it was then that Rose saw something she never saw in any dog she had ever rescued—a smile. It didn't just look like a smile. It *was* a smile.

"Bob, she smiled at me," Rose said in disbelief. "She really smiled."

"I know," he said over his shoulder. "How did you think I knew she wasn't a biting dog? She smiled at me from inside that van, like she knew she was on to better things."

"You never told me that," she said, coming up to them, squatting and rubbing Jamie's furry head.

"You would have never believed me, Rose. It's something you had to have seen on your own."

And he was right. Even having seen it, she still couldn't believe it. Jamie, the smiling dog, had found her true master. But best of all, the man who had once turned away from ever having an animal in his life again, had become an animal lover. Just like Rose. Imagine that.

✿ ✿ Epilogue

"Bob," Rose announced late one May afternoon, coming through the front door after a day at the market. "I've been thinking." She walked over and planted a kiss on his forehead.

"Uh-oh." Bob looked up from the newspaper he was reading on the couch, where he was surrounded by Lucy, Wiggles, Mutt, Annie, Pepper, Agatha, the new puppy, and Jamie, the latest addition to their animal brood. She looked around, not seeing Valentine who was probably in her usual spot by the fridge.

"What? No welcome home?" she called to the dogs.

They all immediately scrambled up and started barking, surrounding her and jumping on her. "I've missed you guys so much," she cooed, rubbing each furry head that came her way.

"So tell me what you've been thinking," Bob said, still sitting on the couch. "Tell me you aren't planning to open that shelter you told me about last night?"

"You know I want to but I don't have the money for it

yet," Rose commented. "I've got to start saving for it. Then, maybe one day..."

"Here." He smiled and took out his passbook from his pocket. "The first deposit."

She embraced him. "You are the best husband in the world!"

"And you're the best wife," he said hugging her back. "So, tell me your new plan."

"Well," she paused and smiled at him. "I've been thinking you and I should take a second honeymoon."

"A second honeymoon?"

"Yeah. We haven't gone anywhere together in a long, long time."

"Well, that's true enough. So what did you have in mind?" he asked.

She shyly smiled. "Just a little getaway in the country for you and me. It'll only be for a few days. I figured since you won't be on the road until next week, we could spend the next couple of days together."

"Wait a second—what about our dogs?"

"That's the good thing about school vacations. Emily and Margaret can stay here with them. I've already asked them and since they finished their final exams, they're free to do it. So what do you think?"

He eyed her suspiciously. "Are you sure you can handle time away from feeding your strays and rescuing dogs?"

"Definitely. Like I said, it's only a few days."

"Let's do it." He smiled and drew her back into his arms. "I'm ready to go right now."

"All ready to go?" Bob asked, walking into the bedroom.

Rose zipped up her bag and smiled at him. "All packed. I just have to make one quick phone call before we go."

"Okay." He picked up her bag. "I'll be waiting outside for you."

She reached for the phone and dialed.

A quiet voice answered. "Hello."

"Mike? Hi! It's Rose."

"Hi!" he said perking up. "I'm so glad it's you. I was just going to call you."

"Really? What's up?"

"Well, there's a hungry looking pack of dogs nearby. And I saw a cop car. I don't know if the cop saw the dogs but if he did... Can you come and help them?"

Rose hesitated. "I'm sorry, Mike. I can't. Actually, I was calling to tell you I'm going out of town. I was going to ask you to keep an eye on the neighborhood dogs for the next few days."

"Oh," he responded unhappily.

She felt terrible letting the little boy down. "Mike, I'm so sorry. I wish I could come right down and help, but I'm literally on my way out the door. My husband's waiting at the car right now."

"Well, have fun on your trip," he said, trying to conjure up some enthusiasm. "It's okay. Don't worry. I'll keep an eye on things."

"Thanks, Mike. I'll call first thing when I get back."

After she hung up, she still felt awful. She couldn't let Bob know she was upset. After all, this trip was her idea. She wanted them both to enjoy it. She took a deep breath, tried to push Dalton City's dogs to the back of her mind, and headed down to the car.

Emily was standing at the front door. As if she could read Rose's mind she told her, "Don't worry about the dogs. We'll take good care of them. Just go and have fun on your second honeymoon!" Emily hugged Rose.

If only Emily knew which dogs Rose was worried about at the moment. She forced a smile. "Thanks, honey. We will!"

Bob helped her into the passenger seat, then came around to the driver's side. "Off we go," he said, climbing into the van. "Boy, I thought I'd never see the day we both would find time to get away together."

He started the car and they headed south. "If only we could have gone to Hawaii or some tropical island," he mused.

Rose looked out her window but didn't respond.

"Then again, with everything that's happened over the past few months, we're lucky we can afford a road trip."

She remained silent.

"Are you worried about the girls or the dogs?" he joked.

Finally, Rose turned to face him. The expression she wore told Bob something was not right.

"What's the matter?"

After a moment, she said, "Never mind. It's nothing."

"Rose? It's obviously not nothing."

She sighed. "I feel bad, that's all."

"Bad about what?"

She just looked at him.

"Come on, you can tell me."

"You know the phone call I made just before we left?"

"Sure."

"I called Mike. I just wanted to tell him I wouldn't be around for a couple of days. You know, so he could keep an eye on things."

"So, why do you feel bad?"

"Well, he was just about to call me. Apparently, he saw a pack of stray dogs in the neighborhood and then he saw a police car. He's scared of what might happen to the dogs. He asked me to come help and I said no. I feel terrible for letting that little boy down. Not to mention the dogs that need help."

The van was quiet for a few minutes. Finally, she said, "I'm being silly. I should just enjoy this trip and not think about strays or Dalton City for a few days."

"You know, we could stop and say good-bye to Mike in person," Bob said, eying her. "It's not that far out of the way."

It was like he could read her mind. He knew exactly what she needed to hear. So much had changed between them. For him to care, no less know exactly how she felt, was the blessing she had always sought. "I know we shouldn't," she murmured. "This is supposed to be our time."

"Yeah, but what's a couple of hours this afternoon? We

still have three days ahead of us. We can be a little late driving to Madison."

Rose looked at him, unsure of what she should do. Bob had sacrificed so much for her these past few months, not to mention for the dogs: his quiet lifestyle, her time with him, the orderliness of their household, even becoming a vegetarian. How could she be so selfish as to take away his first vacation in years? But then again, how could she turn away from animals in need and a boy who saw her as a role model?

"Don't look at me like that with those puppy-dog eyes," Bob said. "All you have to say is let's go and we're there."

"I love you, Bob."

"I know that."

She squirmed in her seat a few moments longer.

"Rose?" he said gently.

She couldn't take it any longer. "I wouldn't forgive myself if something happened to those dogs. We have to go."

"Then that's that," Bob said, turning the corner and heading back toward Dalton City. "It won't take too long."

Rose leaned over and kissed his cheek. "I guess you could say we can't resist a doggie rescue."

"I guess you could say I can't resist you," Bob said, returning her kiss and then pressing down on the gas pedal.

They drove in silence, but united now in heart and mind. All because of a few canine capers.

"We're almost there, sweetheart," Bob reported twenty minutes later, taking a sharp left.

Rose sighed happily. "Hold on, little doggies, here we come."

❖ ❖ Afterword

Rose Block continues to rescue and feed abandoned, abused and stray dogs. She has developed a cooperative and friendly working relationship with local shelters, the Humane Society and the police, all of whom aid her when possible and call her for assistance. But it is the little things—educating owners on dogs and their care, paying for pet medical care when owners can't afford it and taking dogs to the vet for elderly and disabled owners—that have made Rose a much-loved hero of pet lovers in the community where she carries on her crusade.